GOD WANTS YOU WHOLE

GOD WANTS YOU WHOLE

Selwyn Hughes

KINGSWAY PUBLICATIONS

EASTBOURNE

ISBN 0 86065 251 3

AV = Authorized Version
crown copyright

NIV = New International Version
© New York International Bible Society
1978

RSV = Revised Standard Version
copyright 1946, 1952, © 1971, 1973 by
the Division of Christian Education of
the National Council of the Churches of
Christ in the USA

TLB = The Living Bible
© Tyndale House Publishers 1971

PHILLIPS = The New Testament in Modern English
translated by J. B. Phillips, © J. B.
Phillips 1958, 1960, 1972

Front cover design: Vic Mitchell

Printed in Great Britain for
KINGSWAY PUBLICATIONS LTD
Lottbridge Drove, Eastbourne, E. Sussex BN23 6NT by
Cox & Wyman Ltd, Reading.
Typeset by Nuprint Services Ltd, Harpenden, Herts.

Contents

Preface

I set out to write this book five years ago, but when my wife Enid was taken ill with what is known in medical science as Simmond's Disease, I promptly abandoned it.

I said to myself, 'I can hardly write a book on the subject of healing when my own wife is sick. I'll wait until she is better—then write it.'

But Enid did not get better. Now, five years later, there is little evidence of healing. In fact, her doctors have diagnosed that, in addition to Simmond's Disease (a problem in the pituitary gland that affects the distribution of hormones in the body), she has pernicious anaemia and pancreatitis.

A good deal of prayer has gone up for Enid. Hundreds pray for her daily, yet she is unhealed. Her courage and determination not to let her sickness incapacitate her fills me with admiration. She tries to go about her duties uncomplainingly, and is a constant source of inspiration to friends and family alike. Her sickness is not being healed, but it is certainly being used.

Over the past few months, however, I have felt the Lord impressing me to complete this book. And, believe me, it has not been easy. At times the devil has whispered in my ear, 'How can you say *that* when your own wife is sick?' Or, 'You talk about the power of faith—then where is your own?'

I have been tempted to lay the manuscript aside and move on to another subject, but one conviction, reinforced day after day by the Holy Spirit, has kept me going—*God's word is true, no matter how circumstances or situations may argue against it.*

Although I have prayed, and exercised as much faith as I have in relation to Enid's condition, I am not able to explain why, up to this moment, my wife has not been healed. Over the thirty-four years I have been a minister, I have seen God work countless physical miracles in the lives of people. I have prayed for hundreds of people, and seen them miraculously restored to health. But my prayers for my wife seem to be unavailing.

Quite frankly, I do not know *all* the reasons why some are healed and others are not. Some of the reasons are clear to me, while others are still unrevealed. Doubtless we will have to wait until eternity to fully comprehend the reasons why, for some people, healing does not come. 'The subject of healing,' said a preacher, 'is one of the greatest mysteries in the universe. We are big enough to ask the questions, but not big enough to understand the answers.'

I believe that when we arrive in heaven and look back over our earthly pilgrimage, we will see quite clearly the reasons why, despite the most fervent prayers and exercise of faith, some sicknesses refuse to budge. And we shall discover, I suspect, that mostly the reasons had to do with our spiritual dullness, our deep insensitivity and our inability to interpret correctly and apply the scriptural principles for healing.

One thing is clear as we open up the Scriptures: *God is both willing and eager to heal.* This truth runs like a golden thread from Genesis to Revelation. Based on the fact that Scripture is true (even when it conflicts with human life and experience), I have set out in this book to lay down a biblical rationale for the subject of healing, health and wholeness.

Honesty compels me to admit, however, that I present this book with mixed feelings. How I wish I could have added a personal testimony to my wife's healing. I take my stand, however, not on my feelings or my desires, but on the solid, impregnable word of God.

SELWYN HUGHES

1 Three Days to Live

I lay on my back in the city of Sheffield utterly stunned and bewildered. My doctor had told me that unless something dramatic happened, I had less than three days to live.

For weeks I had hovered between life and death with a dangerously high temperature that stubbornly refused to come down. I felt weak and exhausted—unable even to lift a cup of water to my mouth. The doctor came and went, looking graver every time he left the house.

The year was 1958. I had come to the city in connection with my work as a minister and an evangelist. One night, following the regular Sunday evening evangelistic service I conducted in the City Hall, I was struck down with a strange illness that completely mystified the doctor who attended me. At first he diagnosed double pneumonia but, after conferring with his colleagues, he told me that it was far more complex than that.

For several hours after receiving the news that I was soon to die I tried to put my thoughts in some kind of order. I remember thinking: what will happen to my wife, Enid, and my two young children, David, aged seven, and John, just a few months old? Why should God permit me to depart this life at the age of thirty,

11

when my ministry was really only just beginning? Must I resign myself to the situation and accept it as the will of God?

I reached out a feeble hand to the Bible at my bedside and slowly turned its pages hoping that some text or passage might leap out at me and provide me with the comfort I needed. I found myself reading chapter 10 of John's Gospel (AV) but, owing to my weakened condition, the words made little sense. Then my eyes rested on verse 10. I read: 'The thief cometh not, but for to steal, and to kill, and to destroy: I am come that they might have life, and that they might have it more abundantly.'

Somehow the words seemed to burn into my brain. I felt as if my head was spinning. An explosion seemed to take place deep within me, and for several minutes my whole body appeared to be flooded with divine power.

I looked again at the words before me: 'The thief cometh not, but for to steal, and to kill, and to destroy.' I thought, 'The "thief" here refers to the devil. It is *he*, not God, who delights in destroying human life and potential. And it is *he*, not God, who has brought me down into this distressing sickness. Jesus has come to bring life, and it is his life I now feel throbbing through my being.'

That insight might not appear to be particularly meaningful as you read these lines in plain black and white, but to me, who had been brought up to believe that sickness was sent from God as a punishment or as a pruning process to improve one's character, it came with all the force of a blinding revelation.

The words that I had read in John 10:10, although so apparently simple, became, at that moment, positively staggering in their implications. They made such a deep impression that every nerve and cell of my being was powerfully affected.

In a matter of seconds those words of Scripture shattered my preconceived ideas concerning sickness and overturned many of my traditional beliefs. I concluded: God hasn't made me sick—the whole thing is the work of Satan.

The idea of Jesus Christ being the author of abundant life so took hold of me that it cast its healing influence over my entire physical frame. The negative idea of sickness being God's purpose was cast out of my mind. I rose up from my bed perfectly healed and walked around my bedroom with my hands in the air, shouting the praises of God.

My wife, who at that time was downstairs, bravely trying to cope despite the fact that she knew her husband was dying, came running upstairs and stared at me in amazement. She told me later that, as she had never seen anyone die before, she thought that this was the way Christians always behave just prior to going to glory!

'What's happened?' she said.

'I'm healed,' I replied. 'God just touched me when I was reading John 10:10.' She seemed unable to take it in. Then we both burst into tears. We hugged, we cried, we laughed and we thanked the Lord for the demonstration of his healing power.

A little later, my wife informed me that our younger son, John, was seriously ill also. Fearing that the news of his illness might have added to my problems, she had kept it from me. Without hesitation, I walked into the room where John was lying, placed my hands upon him, and prayed that God would heal him. Within an hour his coughing stopped, his temperature came down to normal and the vomiting ceased.

Early next morning, my wife telephoned the doctor to tell him what had happened. He was delighted, of course, and when he came to see me to check on the story, he confessed that he was mystified and nonplussed. I recollect him murmuring something to himself as he walked through the door about 'spontaneous remission'.

'Spontaneous remission'—nonsense! That might be the way medical science explains such an occurrence. In my case, however, the almighty God had intervened in my critical condition, and had touched me with his mighty and miraculous healing power.

In the weeks that followed, I decided not to return to my evangelistic work immediately, but to spend some time thinking through the whole issue of health and wholeness. I spent many long—but rewarding—hours poring over biblical texts and passages in an attempt to construct a theology of healing.

My attitude towards sickness had, until this time, been passive. In my pastoral ministry, whenever anyone came to me to ask for prayer for healing, I would punctuate my prayers with such phrases as, 'Lord, heal this person if it is your will', or 'Teach this person how to bear this sickness for your praise and glory'.

Now, as I studied God's word afresh, and in the light of my own healing, I began to see that there was another way of looking at things. One could adopt a passive attitude towards sickness, or actively resist it and fight it in the strength of God and the power of the Holy Spirit.

There were three well-known biblical passages, however, that I had often used as a defence against those who argued that it was always God's will to heal. In the light of what had happened to me, I approached these passages and examined them in greater depth. I'm glad I did, for the more I pondered them, the more I realized that I had seriously misunderstood their point in Scripture.

Paul's thorn in the flesh

The first passage I examined was the issue of Paul's thorn in the flesh, mentioned in 2 Corinthians 12. I had always believed that Paul's thorn in the flesh was a debilitating sickness or a physical infirmity sent by God to keep the great apostle in a constant state of humility.

This was the way the passage had been interpreted to me by the teachers in the church where I had been brought up, and I clung to it tenaciously. Such an interpretation had in the past enabled me to answer the endless questions that came up in pastoral practice: 'Why am I sick?' or 'Why doesn't God heal me?'

My reply to these questions was: 'If God did not heal the apostle Paul of his sickness when he prayed three times for relief, but instead gave the grace to bear it, then he might have a similar purpose in your life.'

Closer study of this passage, however, led me to reject the view I previously held, that Paul's thorn in the flesh was a physical sickness sent by God to keep him humble. I discovered that the phrase 'thorn in the flesh' was used in the Old Testament in a figurative sense, and always referred to persons, never to things or circumstances.

For example: 'The inhabitants of the land...shall be pricks in your eyes, and thorns in your sides' (Num 33:55, av). Again: 'They shall be...scourges in your sides, and thorns in your eyes' (Josh 23:13, av; see also 2 Sam 23:6).

These statements quite obviously had reference to the people who were going to be extremely hurtful and resistant to the children of Israel when they entered the promised land.

I believe that the apostle Paul, versed in Old Testament theology, used the expression 'thorn in the flesh' to identify not a sickness or a physical disability, but a *personality* who continually harassed him.

And who was that personality? The apostle tells us—
'the *messenger of Satan* set to buffet me'.

In the original Greek the word 'messenger' is *aggelos*,
a word that appears 188 times in the New Testament. It
is translated 181 times as 'angel' and seven times as
'messenger'. It *always* describes a personality and never
an object, a sickness, or a circumstance.

The logical interpretation of what Paul is saying in 2
Corinthians 12 is that, because of his transcendent spiritual experience of being caught up into the third heaven,
a messenger of Satan (an evil spirit) was allowed to
harass him in order that he might maintain his spiritual
balance and be free of arrogance and pride.

The New International Version puts it like this: 'To
keep me from becoming conceited because of these
surpassingly great revelations, there was given me a
thorn in my flesh, a messenger of Satan, to torment me'
(2 Cor 12:7).

The great apostle, having been elevated to the 'third
heaven' and having experienced the glories of paradise,
might well have become spiritually arrogant and proud
had not God permitted him to be harassed by one of
Satan's emissaries.

This fact is borne out by an examination of Paul's
missionary journeys as described in Acts. Wherever the
apostle goes, he encounters hostility and strife. He is
beaten, vilified, imprisoned, outlawed and treated with
contempt. He seems to meet more than his fair share of
trouble. And why? Satan's ambassador was there to
meet him at every twist and turn of his life, stirring up
trouble wherever he went.

There can be little doubt that the messenger of Satan
did his work well, but such was the grace of God that
flowed into the great apostle's life that he was able to

say, 'For the sake of Christ, then, I am content with weaknesses, insults, hardships, persecutions, and calamities' (2 Cor 12:10, rsv).

Once I saw Paul's 'thorn in the flesh' in its proper perspective, I knew that never again would I use it as an illustration of God sending sickness as a way of keeping us humble.

The value of suffering

Having resolved the problems in my mind connected with Paul's 'thorn in the flesh', I turned to think through my second area of concern—the value of suffering. I had always assumed, as a result of the teaching I had received in the early days of my conversion, that the word 'suffering', when used in the Bible, included physical sickness or disability. As a result of this, I entertained the belief that it may not always be God's will for us to be healed, because sickness involves suffering, and suffering has a redemptive value.

How was I to resolve this issue? I set out first to examine what the Bible said about suffering. I studied every text in the Bible that had something to say about the matter. I came across the one that said: 'Although he was a Son, he learned obedience through what he suffered' (Heb 5:8, rsv).

I asked myself: in what way did Christ *suffer*? Was he ever sick? I found the answer to that in Matthew 16:21: 'Jesus began to show his disciples that he must go to Jerusalem and suffer many things from the elders and chief priests and scribes, and be killed, and on the third day be raised' (rsv).

It was plain from this that the suffering Christ endured had to do with his redemptive mission in the world. It was the suffering of misunderstanding, ostracism, hatred

17

and finally the torture of the cross. Through that suffering, he learned obedience to the Father's will, 'and being made perfect he became the source of eternal salvation to all who obey him' (Heb 5:9, RSV).

I then studied the passages in the Bible that speak of the sufferings of those who become followers of the Lord Jesus Christ, and I came across words like these:

> 'We share abundantly in Christ's sufferings' (2 Cor 1:5, RSV).
> 'The apostles left the Sanhedrin, rejoicing because they had been counted worthy of suffering disgrace for the Name' (Acts 5:41, NIV).
> 'Who is going to harm you if you are eager to do good? But even if you should suffer for what is right, you are blessed' (1 Pet 3:13, NIV).
> 'Yea, and all that will live godly in Christ Jesus shall suffer persecution' (2 Tim 3:12, AV).

I came to the conclusion, after examining these and similar passages in the Scriptures, that suffering in the life of a Christian has more to do with the persecution that comes from being a committed follower of Jesus Christ than bearing or carrying a sickness. This is the broad and consistent theme of the Scriptures, and there are no exceptions.

This is not to say, of course, that there are no other meanings to the word 'suffer', such as 'hold up', 'deter' or 'frustrate', but they do not affect the issue. The word 'suffer', when used in relation to a Christian in the New Testament, is not a reference to illness or sickness. Sickness is always sickness and is never described as suffering. And, what is more, Scripture shows that we are to react to it differently. Suffering we accept: sickness we resist.

The apostle James makes this clear in his epistle: 'Is any one of you sick? He should call the elders of the church to pray.... And the prayer offered in faith will make the sick person well' (Jas 5:14–15, NIV).

I remember thinking to myself at this stage of my study: What about all those Christians who say that their sickness brought them nearer to God and made them better Christians? I thought about that long and hard. The conclusion I came to then is still as firm thirty years later: God may not send all things, but he can use all things, even sickness.

It is clear to me from my own study of Scripture that God does not wish sickness upon any of his children, but when it does come, and the Christian responds to the corresponding stream of grace that God supplies, then it can be turned to good account. Any benefit that arises from it is because God works through it to achieve a divine end, not because he purposed it or sent it.

Those who claim that God actually sends sickness because he wants to teach us the value that comes through 'suffering' must remember that there was the same 'value' in it in Jesus' day, yet our Lord never once told those who were sick to 'suffer it a little longer because it is doing you good'. So many times, Scripture says that he healed *all* who came to him.

The biblical trio

Two down, one to go. The next hurdle to be overcome in my mind before I could go out and present a positive healing approach to those to whom God had called me to minister, was the trio of biblical personalities who seemed to have distressing physical problems. I refer to Trophimus, Timothy and Epaphroditus.

The apostle Paul, we read in 2 Timothy 4:20, had left Trophimus 'sick in Miletus' (NIV). In 1 Timothy 5:23, he refers to Timothy's 'frequent illnesses' (NIV). And in

Philippians 2:25–30, he talks about Epaphroditus who nearly died from his illness.

I had often used these scriptures to show that at times it is not always God's will to heal. I also took the line that if healing is guaranteed in response to faith, then surely Paul, a giant in the realm of faith, would have sought and prayed for their recovery.

I began to focus my attention upon these three individuals, one at a time. Taking Epaphroditus first, I reasoned that, although he was sick and healing did not come through the apostle Paul, yet he most certainly recovered, because the Scriptures say quite plainly that 'God had mercy on him'.

Had Epaphroditus violated the laws of health, I wondered, and so brought the sickness upon himself by overwork, lack of sleep or some indiscretion? We will never know for sure, of course, but I can't help feeling that the phrase 'God had mercy on him' is suggestive of the fact that his sickness was one that resulted from a failure to co-operate with the laws of health. Whatever the reason for the delay, however, one thing is sure, healing came to him in due course.

Trophimus, another of Paul's close friends, had been unable to travel with the apostle because he was sick, so he was left at Miletus. Paul, with his great faith and many supernatural gifts, had apparently been unable to restore him to health. Why was this? Did God not want to heal Trophimus? No, for that would be totally inconsistent with the rest of Scripture, which, as we shall see, clearly shows God's great desire to heal.

I concluded that there was some unknown factor in the case of Trophimus that was responsible for his continued sickness, and I felt that, although I would have liked to have known that factor, there were enough positive statements in the Bible to counter the arguments used previously, by myself and others, that Trophimus was sick because God didn't want to heal him.

I came to a similar conclusion concerning the third member of the biblical trio—Timothy. Yet the more I considered Timothy, the more the question of the unknown factor continued to trouble me. Being the type of person who wants clear and precise answers, I found myself in rather a dilemma.

For weeks I struggled with this issue until one day I came across a quotation, the author of which is unknown. I found it on a small sheet of notepaper tucked in one of the pages of a book I had read many times before, but had never noticed. This is what it said:

> If Paul said that three people had not been converted during his ministry in a certain area, would we conclude that it may not be God's will for all men to be saved? Of course not! We would come to our conclusions about the matter based on a broader view of Scripture. We know that it is God's will for all to be saved for he says so: he is not willing that any should perish, but that all may come to repentance (2 Pet 3:9).
>
> Similarly, if Paul says three people were not healed during his ministry, it would be foolish to assume because of this that it is not God's will to heal every one of his children. We would have to remember the broad view of Scripture as evidenced by the ministry of Jesus, and texts like James 5:14, which shows that God delights to heal his children.

Certainly the biblical trio presented me with a number of problems, but the more I considered the matter, the more I was drawn to the conclusion that their experiences made little difference to the clearly established biblical fact that God both delights and is eager to heal.

I know, of course, it is easy to believe what one wants to believe, and because of my own dramatic experience of healing, I had set out to revise my views on the subject. However, the conviction I came to then holds just as firm today. And what is that conviction? Just this: that the experiences of Trophimus, Epaphroditus and Timothy do not in any way qualify the rule and practice of healing in the New Testament.

And the rule and practice is simply this: '*the prayer offered in faith will make the sick person well*' (Jas 5:15, NIV).

Having satisfied myself that the major intellectual doubts I had had about healing were now clearly answered, I felt I had taken the first step towards constructing a theology of healing. I was ready to step out into a new kind of ministry. And what a ministry it turned out to be!

The miracle that God wrought in my life in 1958 launched me into a ministry I never thought possible. It is a ministry through which I have been able to introduce thousands to the fact that God heals today. And not just *physical* healing, but healing in its entirety—healing for the spirit, healing for the soul and healing for the body.

There was another important step, however, that I knew I had to take prior to launching out and sharing the message of supernatural healing with my fellow Christians. I had to hammer out a fuller and broader understanding of God's programme of health and wholeness as contained in both Old and New Testaments.

It took me three months to lay down a biblical foundation for the ministry of healing into which I knew I was about to be drawn. And the foundation I built in those never-to-be-forgotten weeks is what I now want to share with you in the next chapter.

2   Getting a Biblical Perspective

Prior to my dramatic healing in 1958, most of my prayers for healing, whether in relation to myself or others, brought little success. Looking back now I can see quite clearly that my faith for healing was sabotaged from the start by my ambivalent attitude towards sickness.

I was never quite sure how to approach the matter of physical illness. I knew what to do with sin, and that was to resist it with all the force of my being. But sickness? That was different. Sometimes I was against it, sometimes I ignored it and sometimes I tolerated it. This uncertainty undermined my faith.

Following the events that I have described in the previous chapter, it became clear to me that if I wanted to help others over this vitally important matter of healing, then I must have a sound biblical basis.

I went into my study every morning and spent three to four hours perusing the Bible from Genesis to Revelation, trying to gain a deep and clear understanding as to what the Scriptures taught about healing. I asked myself such questions as:

What does God say in his word about the healing of sicknesses, diseases, pains and infirmities, all of which plague mankind?

Is it the will of God to heal the body as well as the soul and spirit?

If it is the prayer of *faith* that heals the sick, then how can faith be developed to its highest potential?

The convictions that grew out of my intensive study at that time have never left me, and they are still as fresh and exciting as I write now, over twenty-five years later.

Permit me to share with you some of the biblical concepts that made me so certain, not only of God's willingness to heal, but of his *eagerness* to heal.

God's great Old Testament promise of healing

In Exodus 15, God gave this great promise to his people, the children of Israel: 'If thou wilt diligently hearken to the voice of the Lord thy God, and...wilt give ear to his commandments, and keep all his statutes, I will put none of these diseases upon thee, which I have brought upon the Egyptians: for I am the Lord that healeth thee' (v.26, AV).

This promise—or, as some Christians refer to it, this *covenant*—was given in a rather interesting context. Having passed safely through the Red Sea, the children of Israel journeyed three days into the wilderness without finding water. When they arrived at Marah and discovered that the water there was unfit to drink, they became greatly dispirited.

God demonstrated his love for them by miraculously causing the water to become pure: 'And the Lord showed him [Moses] a tree, which when he had cast in the waters, the waters were made sweet: there he made for them a statute and an ordinance, and there he proved them' (v.25, AV).

On a later occasion (Exod 23:25–26), God reaffirmed his covenant of healing with his people, and even

24

extended it when he said, 'You shall serve the Lord your God, and I will bless your bread and your water; and I will take sickness away from...you. None shall cast her young or be barren in your land; I will fulfil the number of your days' (RSV).

On the strength of this promise, Moses, when preparing the people for the promised land, sought to encourage their faith by reiterating the words that God had given them regarding healing: 'The Lord will take away from you all sickness; and none of the evil diseases of Egypt....will he inflict upon you' (Deut 7:15, RSV).

It is important to notice something here that is often missed by commentators, namely that God's promise of healing was conditional upon his people's obedience. '*If* thou wilt diligently hearken to the voice of the Lord thy God...*I* will put none of these diseases upon thee.'

Although God willed their health it was clear that in order for his promise to become a reality, *they had to will it too*. God prescribed for his people certain laws which, when obeyed, would protect them from serious sickness and disease. God was not only concerned about healing them when they became ill, but also in preventing them from falling sick.

Let's take a look at one of those preventative laws— one that brings into clear focus the point I am making here. God commanded that if one of the children of Israel touched a dead body, then they should immediately go through a simple ritual of cleansing. This ritual is detailed in Numbers 19:14–19.

One of the things God stipulates in that passage is this: 'and running water shall be added in a vessel' (RSV).

Why 'running water', we might ask? Little was made of this point by Bible commentators until about a hundred years ago when, through the discoveries of Dr Ignaz Semmelweis, the attention of the medical world was drawn to the need for hand washing in *running* water after contact with a dead body.

At that time, Dr Semmelweis observed that one in six women in the maternity wards of the hospital in Vienna where he practised died as a result of childbirth. Obstetricians ascribed their deaths to such things as constipation, delayed lactation, fear and poisonous air.

The young doctor, unconvinced that these were the real causes of death, began in-depth research. He noticed that doctors with their teams of medical students often went from performing autopsies on the dead to making pelvic examinations on the living pregnant women, *without washing their hands*.

In April 1847 he established a rule in his ward that anyone who had been involved in performing an autopsy must carefully wash his hands before examining a live patient. When this practice was observed, the number of deaths dropped dramatically. Similarly, he ordered that everyone should wash their hands after examining each *living* patient, to prevent disease being carried from one patient to another. Although, at the time, many of his colleagues scorned his practice of hand washing and were loathe to accept his findings, the practice gradually came to be recognized as essential.

Dr S. I. McMillen in his book *None of These Diseases*, referring to the matter of Ignaz Semmelweis's discovery, says: 'Such mortality would not have occurred if surgeons had only followed the method God gave to Moses regarding the meticulous method of hand washing and changing of clothes after contact with infectious diseases.... At long last, in the year 1860, man finally muddled through. He learned, after centuries and a frightful cost, what God gave to Moses by *inspiration*.'

The study of God's first promise of healing led me to a firm and definite conclusion: To expect God to heal us when we deliberately ignore the laws he has laid down for our health is the height of impertinence. It is not enough that God wills our health—we must will it too.

Other Old Testament references

It would be impossible, of course, for me to catalogue all the Old Testament references to healing that I studied in those days following my healing, but let me share briefly one or two more.

One passage in particular that came to mean a great deal to me during those days of study (and, indeed, still does!) is the following from Psalm 103: 'Bless the Lord, O my soul, and forget not all his benefits: Who forgiveth all thine iniquities; *who healeth all thy diseases*' (vv.2–3). Here was another indication, I remember thinking, of God's care and concern, not just for the spiritual welfare of his people, but for their physical well-being too.

The Psalmist makes clear here that the one who forgives all our iniquities is the same Lord who heals all our diseases. As forgiveness is offered to all, so is healing offered to all. Those who say healing is not for all ought, logically, to say that forgiveness is not for all.

Another Old Testament passage that occupied my attention was Isaiah 53. Up until this time I had interpreted the words, 'Surely he hath borne our griefs . . . and with his stripes we are healed' (vv.4–5, AV) as having reference only to the spiritual ills of the human race.

I thought of verse 10 in that same way too: 'Yet it pleased the Lord to bruise him; he hath put him to grief . . .' An examination of the words in this passage, with the help of a Bible concordance, enabled me to see that the word 'grief' in the Authorized Version is a translation of the Hebrew word *challah* which means sickness or disease.

According to the Hebrew scholars, the phrase could be interpreted, 'He has put him to grief and made him sick.' It dawned upon me that the prophet Isaiah was telling the world that one day the Suffering Servant would come and lay down his life, not only for the spiritual ills of mankind, but for their physical sicknesses as well.

This interpretation, I discovered, was borne out by Matthew's writing in the New Testament. In chapter 8 of his Gospel, he describes a day in the life of Jesus that was distinguished by the many miracles of healing he did among the people. As Matthew witnessed this, he was given to see by the Spirit that the healing ministry of Christ was in anticipation of his bearing both mankind's sins and sicknesses on the cross.

This is how he puts it: 'He ... healed all that were sick: That it might be fulfilled which was spoken by Esaias the prophet, saying, Himself took our infirmities, and bare our sicknesses' (Mt 8:16–17, AV).

We cannot be sure that Matthew understood the spiritual significance of that verse in Isaiah (i.e. the vicarious sufferings of Christ for the sins of mankind), but we can be sure that he saw its physical significance for he relates the verse, by the Spirit's prompting, to a wholly physical situation.

New Testament references

Having concluded, from a study of the Old Testament scriptures, that God willed the health of his people, I then turned to make a similar study of the New Testament. My first task was to read straight through the four Gospels in an attempt to pinpoint the attitude of Jesus towards sickness.

I discovered, as someone else once pointed out, that

whenever you meet Jesus Christ in the Gospels, he is either on his way to heal someone who is sick, on his way back from healing someone who was sick, or is actually about to heal someone who is sick. One-third of Jesus' ministry was spent in bringing healing to the people of his day. There can be no doubt that relieving mankind of their *physical* as well as spiritual maladies was a significant part of his ministry.

At the very beginning of his mission, he announced the purpose of his being in the world in these dramatic words:

> The Spirit of the Lord is upon me, because he hath anointed me to preach the gospel to the poor; he hath sent me to heal the broken-hearted, to preach deliverance to the captives, and recovering of sight to the blind, to set at liberty them that are bruised (Lk 4:18).

It was obvious from this that the Saviour came into the world to free men and women from the oppression that sin, sickness and disease had brought upon them. It was his manifesto, so to speak, and, as someone has pointed out, this manifesto, unlike those of many modern political parties, was fulfilled in every respect!

I found in the Gospels twenty-six cases of individual healings and ten cases of multiple healings, ranging from small groups to great multitudes of people. I stopped at every passage that recorded one of Jesus' healings and asked myself: What was Jesus' *purpose* in bringing healing to this person or persons?

Three reasons why Jesus healed

I discovered that Jesus healed people for three specific reasons. Firstly, he healed people as a direct expression of the mind and will of God. In the case of the man born blind (Jn 9:4), he said: 'I must work the works of him that sent me' (AV). To the leper (Mk 1:40–41) who said, 'If you will, you can make me clean,' he replied, 'I will; be clean' (RSV).

Secondly, Jesus healed the sick to validate his claim of being the Son of God. This can be seen from the account of the paralytic who was brought to him by friends (Mk 2:1–12). Before healing the man Jesus told him that his sins were forgiven. There were protests, of course, but Jesus replied that the healing miracle he was about to perform was the proof of his power to forgive sins, and confirmation of the fact that he was who he said he was—the Son of the living God.

He had a similar purpose, too, when, in answer to John the Baptist's disciples, who came and asked, 'Are you he who is to come, or shall we look for another?' he said, 'Go and tell John what you hear and see: the blind receive their sight and the lame walk, lepers are cleansed and the deaf hear, and the dead are raised up, and the poor have good news preached to them' (Mt 11:3–5, RSV).

The third reason why Jesus healed the sick was because of his great compassion for them in their suffering. This can be seen in the case of the leper to whom we referred earlier: 'And Jesus, moved with compassion, put forth his hand, and touched him' (Mk 1:41, AV). We see it again in the case of the multitude who followed him out into the desert: 'And Jesus went forth, and saw a great multitude, and was moved with compassion toward them, and he healed their sick' (Mt 14:14).

The thing that impressed me about the healing ministry of Christ was that never once did he turn down a request for healing or say to someone, 'Suffer it a little longer: it's helping to develop your character.'

Someone has pointed out that Jesus didn't give a

Beatitude for sickness, and while we cannot argue from omissions, it is, nevertheless, an interesting observation.

When people came to Christ for healing, he responded, more often than not, without any exposition of spiritual truths. He never once said, 'I am willing to heal you, but you must realize that there is something more important than physical healing.' One writer puts it succinctly when he says, 'Even when Jesus emphasized the spiritual work of redemption, he never did so in any way that minimized the importance of physical healing.'

I shall never forget the thrilling conclusion that impressed itself upon my spirit as I completed my study of the healing ministry of the Gospels: *Jesus healed men and women. He healed them wherever he went. He never failed to heal, and he healed all who came to him.*

The healing ministry of Christ's followers

My next task was to study the ministry of healing as continued by Christ's disciples. Jesus, it appears, spent much time training his disciples to go and continue what he had begun. There are no fewer than five occasions when he made his wishes clear on this matter (Mt 10:7–8, Mk 6:7, Mk 16:17–18, Lk 9:1–2, Lk 10:8–9).

His words obviously had great impact upon them for right through the Acts of the Apostles we read of how his followers taught and practised the ministry of healing that he had begun. The book of Acts records nine cases of individual healing, or miracles, done by the disciples, and refers to multiple healings on seven occasions.

The individual healings are: the crippled man at the gate called Beautiful (Acts 3:1–10), Paul's sight restored (Acts 9:10–19), Aeneas healed of paralysis (Acts 9:32–35), Tabitha restored to life (Acts 9:36–42), the crippled man healed at Lystra (Acts 14:8–10), the girl freed from

31

a spirit of divination (Acts 16:16–18), Eutychus brought back to life (Acts 20:7–12), Paul unharmed by the bite of a viper (Acts 28:3–6) and the father of Publius who was healed of a fever (Acts 28:8).

The multiple healings recorded in Acts are found in Acts 2:43, 5:12–16, 6:8, 8:5–8, 14:3, 19:11–12 and 28:9.

Healing in the epistles

Having satisfied myself that healing was an integral part of Jesus' ministry and that of his disciples, I then turned to the epistles in order to see if the same emphasis was given to the subject there. I discovered that although there were numerous inferences to healing in the epistles, there were just two passages that gave a clear indication that healing is to be a permanent feature of the Christian church's ministry.

The first passage is 1 Corinthians 12:1–11. Here the apostle says that the Holy Spirit divides his ministries among believers, one of those ministries being the gift of healing: 'To another faith by the same Spirit, to another gifts of healing by the one Spirit' (v.9, RSV).

I remembered the argument that often came up in Christian circles whenever the subject of healing was mentioned, namely, that the ministry of supernatural healing in the New Testament was 'dispensational' and ended with the Acts of the Apostles. I had never taken that view, but I was glad to find that this passage made clear the continuity of the healing ministry in the Christian church.

The second passage that gave clear teaching about the ongoing ministry of healing in the church is found in James 5:14–15. This passage shows plainly that the ministry of healing should be an integral part of every community of Bible-believing Christians:

Is any among you sick? Let him call for the elders of the church, and let them pray over him, anointing him with oil in the name of the Lord; and the prayer of faith will save the sick man, and the Lord will raise him up; and if he has committed sins, he will be forgiven (RSV).

The procedure is clear: in response to the sick person's call, the elders of the church are to anoint him with oil and pray the prayer of faith. The prayer of faith will result not only in the person being healed of his physical problems, but it will affect his spiritual life as well through the confession and forgiveness of his sins. This means, quite clearly, that the healing ministry of the church is concerned with more than people just being well. It is concerned about them being whole. As well as the body, there is the need for the mind and spirit to be healed.

This passage in James is the climax to a consistent Old Testament and New Testament revelation: that God delights in and desires his people to be well and whole.

When I concluded my study on healing, I saw the subject in a completely new light. I knew instinctively that no longer would I pray for either my own or someone else's healing with the faith-destroying phrase: 'If it be thy will.'

To me, both then and now, the issue is fundamental— for unless God wills healing, then it is useless to pray for it. If we pray with positive words—'Lord, bring healing to this person in your name'—yet hold a contrary belief in our hearts—'I wonder, do you really want to heal this person, Lord?'—then faith will be sabotaged by doubt.

Although my study of the word of God still left me with intellectual problems concerning healing, the issue of whether sickness is the will of God was for ever settled. Not once, since the moment I ended my special study of the Scriptures, have I ever changed, or been tempted to change, that view. This is not to say that at times I do not wrestle with difficulties concerning the matter of healing, but the conviction that God does not will sickness is firm and unshakeable.

I hope that I have persuaded you of that too!

3 'There Ought to Be a Law'

One of the things that has increasingly fascinated me since the day God miraculously healed me is to find that the principle of healing is not only written into the texts of Scripture, but into the very texture of our physical constitution. It is found not only in the Bible, but in the warp and woof of human biology.

Bernard, a famous biologist, said, 'All the mechanisms of the body have one object...to bring about stability in the organism. If there is hurt or injury, and providing there are no great complications, the body leaps toward correcting the problems.' J. S. Hadfield comments, 'No more pregnant statement was ever framed by a biologist.'

Ever heard someone say, 'There ought to be a law...'? People use that expression when they feel there ought to be a clear principle governing a difficult or confusing situation. You may think that the matter of healing can be so perplexing (after all, there are those who say God sometimes wants to heal yet sometimes he doesn't) that there ought to be a law governing its interpretation.

Well there is! The law of healing runs throughout the entire universe. It can be found in the tiniest cells of our bodies, and it says, 'Life that is hurt or injured is designed to heal or repair itself.'

You hardly need me to tell you that the entire universe is sustained by laws. Take the law of gravity, for example. Because of it, we can move about the earth's surface in comparative safety. If, for some reason, it was suspended, then we would fly off the earth's surface into outer space!

Imagine a housewife in a kitchen where the law of gravity did not operate. Life would be very difficult indeed, for it is this law that keeps everything in its place. Pots and pans would fly around, and refuse to stay where they are put—it would be complete chaos. Or picture a husband trying to build a cabinet in a workshop where gravity was suspended. What effect would his hammer have on the nails? That is, if he could ever catch them!

In biology there are laws too. You never see half a dog or half a cat. It is true that a law can sometimes be set aside temporarily, for example, a horse can be crossed with a donkey to produce a mule. But the mule will not breed. There's a law.

Illustrations of God's law at work in the universe can be drawn from all fields: science, physics, hygiene, botany, chemistry and so on. God's laws function all the time, day and night, in accordance with a prearranged design he laid down from the foundation of the world.

The law of healing at work

The law of healing is, in my view, one of the most fascinating laws in the universe. Watch it at work. Break a branch off a small tree, and some weeks later what do you find? The tree has healed itself.

A small burl will have appeared at the place where the branch was broken off because the tree has a built-in healing ability put there by the Creator. As soon as the break occurred, the tree set about healing itself. Why

36

did the tree respond in this way? Because the law of healing went to work.

Take another example, this time from the world of animals. An animal in a forest is wounded in a fight and because there is no one to care for it or take it to a vet, it slinks away to a quiet spot to await the healing that inevitably comes. Whenever something living is wounded, the law of healing goes to work.

The same thing takes place in the human body. A man nicks his face while shaving. Does he panic? No. He knows that, within minutes, the blood will clot, and the cut will start to heal itself right away.

A similar thing happens when a woman cuts herself with a potato knife. Is she shattered by the accident? Hardly. She slips a Band-Aid on her finger, and providing she has enough vitamin K in her body, the cut will heal perfectly in a matter of days. You see—there's a law.

The law of healing, resident in the human frame, can perform some amazing feats. In recent years, we have heard of the discovery of interferon, a miracle drug that will (so some think) cure all kinds of diseases from the common cold to cancer. Until recently the only source of interferon was the human body itself, and at this moment medical scientists are exploring ways in which they can produce it synthetically.

Think about it. The human body has the built-in capacity for producing interferon, this mysterious chemical that has such powerful healing properties. I wonder what other mysteries lie within the physical frame that God has given us.

The more I ponder the amazing law of healing that God has placed within the human body, the more I understand the statement of the doctor who said, 'The closer I examine the human body, and the more I study its built-in ability to fight sickness and disease, *I wonder*

37

how anyone gets sick' (italics mine).

The law of healing written in the DNA

One of the great discoveries of our generation is what scientists call 'the code of life'. This is an exquisite and astonishing structure called DNA, a handy nickname for deoxyribonucleic acid (translated: 'an acid in the nuclei of cells, made of deoxidized sugar'). This single molecule, say our scientists, *is life itself*.

Forgive me if I get a little technical in the next few paragraphs, but your personal DNA has a vivid memory that time does not dim. It houses a vast number of directions and blueprints, which it issues at the right time and place to trigger the building of all the cells and structures of the body, make them grow and synchronize their operations at every second during their allotted life.

The DNA molecule consists of threads so thin that they can only be seen under a powerful electron microscope. Yet, when stretched out, each of these strands can measure up to 6 feet in length. The DNA has a simple form. It consists of two intertwined tape-like coils, connected by cross-pieces at regular intervals—like a spiral staircase. This it can shorten and elongate, compress and open up by coiling and uncoiling.

There is surprising logic in the long, slender form of the DNA, say the scientists, for this gives it the capacity, like magnetic recording tape, for storing the vast quantity of information needed in a lifetime. It has been estimated that if all the instructions impressed in the DNA were put into English letters, they would fill a 1,000-volume encyclopedia!

The coded directions in your DNA were compiled by selection from those of your mother and father at your conception. That first cell, believe it or not, was a complete you. It held advance reservations for all the bodily functions of your life.

From the beginning of your conception, the coded instructions in your personal DNA began to tell the cell to divide. This is the way all living things grow—by cellular division. A cell splits into two. Then the daughter cells divide again, so there are four. The four become eight, and so on. With each division, the number of cells double until the process has produced billions upon billions of cells.

Along with the production of cells, various organs begin to take shape, the first one being the brain. The brain, of course, is a living organism, but it can best be described as an amazing computer, far more complex and intricate than anything produced by man. It is composed of 10 billion cells (neurons) that never sleep. This living computer has more than 500 trillion connections in its circuitry called synapses.

All of the instructions of the DNA go into this computer that we call the brain, and then the brain takes over the responsibility of seeing that they are carried out. One of the instructions the DNA puts into the brain's computer is the message that should the body ever become ill or invaded by germs, then a defence system must go into operation right away to restore the balance of the body and keep the organism functioning as perfectly as possible.

The law of healing is written in the DNA of the first cell of our being. Those almost invisible threads contain complete instructions for the growth and maintenance of the human body, including the healing process.

Now I ask you, can you survey this amazing process without coming to the inevitable conclusion that God longs for us to be well? The more I consider this, the more it fires my spirit to pray for health and healing in my own body as well as those of others. When we realize that God has designed us for health, and that he desires us to be whole, it makes a tremendous difference to our confidence when approaching him in prayer.

Make no mistake about it, whatever the reasons for any sickness that exists in your life (and later we shall examine some of those reasons), the message that comes both from the texts of Scripture and from the texture of life is that God wants you to be well.

Repairs and defence

When David, the Psalmist, said, 'I am fearfully and wonderfully made', he didn't tell the half of it. Consider the way God has designed the body to repair and defend itself in times of sickness or danger. Every day our bodies are assailed by millions of germs, many of which can produce illness or death.

Yet more often than not, we remain well. Countless bacteria and viruses gain entry into our bodies with the food we eat or the air we breathe, or through injury or damage to our skin. Some of these, say scientists, establish permanent residence in the mouth or nose where they multiply at a fantastic rate—yet usually to no great detriment to us.

Why is this? What protects us from these ceaseless assaults by bacteria and viruses?

The answer is that our health is safeguarded by an ingenious series of defences, arranged like the successive lines of an army entrenched to ward off invaders. When an invader does get through, then an amazing repair system immediately goes into action—a repair system programmed into the body by the Creator himself.

Suppose, for example, a germ-laden speck of dust gets

into your eye. Usually there is no need to worry because your eye manufactures a tear which contains a bacteria-destroying antiseptic called lysozyme.

Lysozyme is so powerful that a single teardrop, diluted with half a gallon of water, will still destroy at least one species of germs. Our saliva, together with other fluids manufactured by the body, also contains antiseptic chemicals. Even our bare skin has considerable germi-cidal power. Virulent dysentery bacteria in a drop of fluid on a glass slide will survive for hours, while those in a drop placed in the palm of a clean hand will be dead in about twenty minutes.

Sometimes a person catches a cold that turns into pneumonia. Today, powerful drugs can be administered that deal with the problem in a few days, but catch a glimpse of what the body can do on its own. Once the virus or bacteria becomes active in the body, a signal is sent to the brain, whose computer mobilizes the defen-sive forces of the body towards action.

Our bodies have a built-in identification system that *labels* invading germs or viruses. These labels, which attach themselves to the invaders, are called antibodies. Most cases of recovery from an infection are traceable largely to the action of antibodies. In about nine days (that's about how long it takes for the body to complete its preparations), the organism is ready to make a deter-mined assault on the virus.

The person suffering from the virus knows nothing of what is going on in the body because it all takes place automatically. But right on cue, when the body's preparations are complete, the two foes meet and battle begins. This is usually called 'the crisis' time, and if the system has been able to produce enough antibodies, the virus will be destroyed and the person's health restored.

Could we survive without this amazing law of healing

that is resident within the human frame? It seems unlikely.

All bodily mechanisms work towards one end: stability

The French physiologist, Dr Charles Richet, says, 'The healthy living being is stable. If it lacks that, it perishes. It must be in order to avoid being destroyed by the colossal forces, often adverse, which surround it.'

We have already seen something of the body's marvellous ability to restore itself when it is hurt or injured owing to the fact that the Almighty has written into our physical frame an amazing law of healing and health. Now we shall see how our bodies adapt to maintain stability whenever we are injured.

When skin, muscles, blood vessels or bones are injured, the organism immediately adapts itself in an effort to maintain stability. For instance, when an artery is cut, blood gushes out, and arterial pressure is lowered. The patient feels a sudden faintness. The haemorrhage decreases, and a clot of fibrin forms in the wound. Then the haemorrhage stops. During the next few days leucocytes and tissue cells invade the clot, and progressively regenerate the wall of the artery.

When a limb is fractured, sharp pieces of the broken bone may tear muscles and blood vessels. The body reacts and sets about restoring a balance. The torn muscles and blood vessels are surrounded by a haemotoma—a clot of blood. Circulation becomes more active. The limb swells. The nutritive substances, vital to the regeneration of the tissues, are brought into the wounded area. Everything focuses on completing the repair.

Dr Cannon, the Harvard physiologist to whom I owe so much in the writing of this chapter, says, 'The nervous system is divisible into two main parts: the one acting outwardly and affecting the world around us, and the other acting inwardly and helping to preserve a constant and steady condition of the organism itself.'

This points once more to the fact that there is a law within us that goes into action whenever the stability of the body is endangered. In an experiment a man drank six quarts of water in six hours. The rate of kidney output rose to one and a quarter quarts per hour. And yet in tests of the blood during the period no appreciable dilution could be observed. The laws that God has built into the body saw to it that the normal constitution of the blood was maintained.

Nature not only takes care of the vital centres out of the body's current supplies and resources, but lays up supplies for emergencies. The water supply in the body is vital. The average person has about a hundred pounds of water. The grey matter in the brain is 80% water, and blood plasma is 90% water.

When we fast we can lose practically all our stored animal starch or glycogen without harmful consequences. We can lose all our reserves of fat and about half the protein that is stored in our body structure without great danger. But a loss of 10% of body water is serious and 20—25% means certain death.

So water is kept in reservoirs throughout the body and liberated as and when it is needed. Yes, it is an established fact—the goal of all the organisms is stability.

Doctors depend on the healing principle

A saying that I'm sure you have heard goes like this: 'The doctor may dress the wound, but only God can heal it.' No doctor or physician ever healed anyone. God alone heals.

Whenever healing occurs, in a medical sense, it is

because men have aligned themselves with the laws of the human organism. Every doctor, every nurse, every medical specialist must co-operate with the healing principle in some way. Healing cannot occur apart from it.

As one doctor put it, 'No intelligent physician of any school claims to do more than assist the natural forces of the body to restore a person to health.'

Some time ago a member of my family underwent a serious operation. He was told that the doctor who performed it was a Christian. When the operation was over and he had recovered from the anaesthetic, the doctor appeared at his bedside and said, 'I removed the blockage and I sewed up everything the way it should be—*now it's up to the Lord.*'

Once a doctor has completed an operation in which he has removed a blockage, or taken away a diseased organ, or remedied an internal disorder, then the patient has to sit back and wait for the body's mechanisms of healing to take over and finish the job. And the point of this statement? Simply to reinforce what I have already said: no doctor can heal. The healing occurs only because the Lord has established a wonderful healing process in the body.

Are you now convinced that God wants you well? I most certainly am. The more I examine the Bible and the more I understand the functioning of the human frame, the deeper my conviction gets that God is on the side of health, and his will is that we be well.

The staggering design of the human constitution, with its built-in ability to bring about balance and stability through an almost endless defence and repair system, leaves me nearly breathless with wonder.

Make no mistake about it—God wants you well. If that is not his purpose, then why should he have taken such pains to create such an astonishing healing system in the human body?

Pain: first signal of danger

Another amazing ability with which God has equipped us is the ability to feel pain. 'Pain', said the late Dr Sangster, 'is the monitor of human health. It rings a warning bell at the slightest approach of danger, and although many people wish it could be eliminated, it is, in fact, one of the greatest blessings of life.'

According to two journalists, Ruth and Edward Brecher, writing in an issue of the *Reader's Digest*, a young woman named Lucy, who lives in Western Canada, was born without any sense of pain. It is said that she has never felt an ache or a pain in her life.

But you wouldn't envy Lucy if you knew her. Her body is a mass of bruises and scars. Because she lacked the warning signals that pain provides, she has several times suffered serious burns, broken bones and other disabilities.

When our bodies experience a twinge of pain, they respond in a number of ways. Blood is re-routed to the brain, lungs and muscles: our hearts beat faster, blood pressure rises—all preparations for taking action, not against the pain, but against the cause of it.

Our liver secretes stored-up sugar into our bloodstream, and this energy-providing chemical is rapidly carried to the muscles. If the pain is due to an injury to the head, tears probably flow, the nose runs—all of which is the body's way of getting rid of harmful substances.

If the pain is from an internal source, an entirely different set of protective responses is triggered. Blood pressure drops, nausea and other unpleasant symptoms make us want to lie down—an excellent position for recovery.

Have you ever exercised to the point where your muscles felt acute pain? If you stop exercising, in a few days the pain will die away, but if you start exercising again too early, the pain will again become acute. It is nature's way of telling you to hold off for a while. The muscles need a rest.

The sensory nerve system, which alerts the body to pain and danger, is distributed through our bodies in accordance with an intelligible plan, thought up by none other than our Creator.

Doctors Hardy and Wolff classified pain into three types. One they described as 'prickly' pain: this reaches our consciousness immediately after our skin is cut, bruised or scalded. It is sharp and tells you precisely where the hurt or injury occurred.

A second type of pain is a 'burning' pain: this is a dull pain which lasts longer and spreads over a wide area.

The third type of pain is what they describe as an 'aching' pain: it arises from the nerve endings in our internal structure rather than the skin.

These classifications of pain arose out of laboratory tests, but the actual pain we experience in real life may be much more acute owing to such things as worry, fear, apprehension, dread and other emotional factors that can be mixed in with it.

Each of us reacts differently to pain, too. A boxer who ignores even the most intense pain in the ring may cry like a baby in a dentist's chair. And a football or rugby player who may be seriously hurt at some stage of the game may feel little or nothing until some time later.

Experiments have shown that the intensity of pain does not depend upon the amount of tissue that is injured, but on the rate at which it is injured. If we immerse our bodies in hot water, which stays at a constant temperature of 112 degrees Fahrenheit for a period of six hours, we will feel only a moderate degree of pain. Yet, at the end of the period, we will be thoroughly cooked.

Conversely, if a white-hot iron were to touch our skin for a fraction of a second, we would suffer excruciating pain although it might not even produce a burn.

We often suspect that some people are less sensitive to pain than others, but research says this isn't so. Generally, people experience pain in about the same degree. Some just make less fuss about it. Two doctors have demonstrated this by means of a pain thermometer called a 'dolorimeter' from the Latin word for pain—*dolor*.

Each degree on the 'dolorimeter' is defined as 1 'dol'. A pinprick, or any other slight pain that one barely feels, is half a dol. An ordinary headache may be measured as 2 or 3 dols. The pain experienced during the passing of a kidney stone measures 10½ dols. And 10½ dols, by the way, is the ceiling for pain. Pain never rises above this level, say the doctors concerned, even though the cause of the pain continues to increase in intensity.

Some people can stand an 8 dol pain with more fortitude than someone who experiences a 2 or 3 dol pain. And there are those, of whom any dentist will tell you, who react to a 1 dol pain as if they were being run over by a steamroller!

Sometimes surgeons perform nerve cutting operations to quieten pains that yield to no other treatment. The difficulty they encounter is that often the source of the pain isn't where it appears to be. To avoid being fooled by this, a surgeon temporarily paralyses a nerve with injections before cutting it. If the pain disappears he knows that he has located the correct nerve. Needless to say, this kind of surgery is a last resort.

Our aches and pains, like the sights and sounds we hear, are an important part of our constitution. They are the part of our Creator's design which enables us to deal with causes rather than symptoms. For this reason, among others, it is important to see them as loving intentions and not hateful ones.

How ingenious of God to build into our systems this sensitivity to pain. And how fitting, too, that he made it impossible for us to turn off this sensitivity by an act of will. We may not like pain, but how necessary it is to efficient functioning.

Imagine what would happen if we could push a button and turn off our susceptibility to pain. Without the warning that pain gives, we would tear our hands to pieces using them as wrenches, or burn them handling items too hot for us to bear. Our hands would become useless in no time at all.

The Great Physician knew that we have neither the wisdom nor the restraint to be in charge of the body's regulatory system. So he made it impossible for us to turn it off.

What a Creator!

4   Why, Then, Do We Get Sick?

If the human organism is so evidently designed to be healthy, why, then, do we get sick? That is the question we must come to grips with in this chapter.

There is no doubt that the issue of sickness and disease is one of the most disturbing problems in the universe. Studdart Kennedy used to say that a man who was undisturbed by the problem of sickness and disease was suffering from one of two things: either a hardening of the heart, or a softening of the brain.

Kennedy was right. Everyone who is mentally alert and alive finds this problem difficult to solve. But, as we have seen, one thing is certain—God does not *will* disease. He may permit it in his universe, just as in the same way he has permitted sin, but it is not part of his purpose or his design.

Sickness, like sin, is an intrusion in God's universe, and it is only when we see it in those terms that we can have the proper attitude towards it.

Some people would like to lay the blame for the problem of sickness and disease at God's door. In his autobiography, Sir Arthur Conan Doyle tells what made him an agnostic early in life:

I was called by a woman to see her daughter. She pointed to a cot in the humble sitting room. I picked up a candle and walked over. A pair of brown sullen eyes, full of loathing and pain looked up at me. I could not tell how old the creature was. Long, thin limbs were twisted and coiled on the tiny couch. The face was sane, but malignant. 'What is it?' I asked in dismay. 'It's a girl,' sobbed the mother. 'Oh, if only God would take her.'

In the presence of such problems answers don't come easily. But I affirm again that God is not the author of such situations. Whatever purposes God might have in permitting such horrifying things to take place, I want to state once again, as firmly and as categorically as I can, that God does not *intend* such suffering. He permits it, yes. And he can turn sickness and suffering to good, just as he can with sin, but he does not *will* them. Disease of the body is no more the will of God than disease of the soul.

From a Lambeth Conference of the Church of England, which took place in the first half of this century, came this statement: 'However disease may be brought about, and whatever way it may be over-ruled for good, it is in itself an evil.' If it is true that sickness and disease are not the result of some decree of the Almighty, then where does this problem originate? Where do we look to trace the origin of this malady that has come upon mankind?

As I see it, there are three answers to that question:

1. Sickness and disease came upon humanity as a direct result of Adam and Eve's transgression in the Garden of Eden

Profound words about the original creation of man leap out at us from the opening pages of Genesis. 'Male and female created he them; and blessed them, and called their name Adam, in the day when they were created' (Gen 5:2, AV). The Almighty, we are told, placed the first human pair in a beautiful garden surrounded by everything they needed, but despite his evident love and care, they insisted on having their own way, and rebelled against his instructions not to eat of the fruit of 'the tree of the knowledge of good and evil':

> And the Lord God commanded the man, saying, Of every tree of the garden thou mayest freely eat: But of the tree of the knowledge of good and evil, thou shalt not eat of it (Gen 2:16–17, AV).

Eve, afraid she was missing out on something, responded to Satan's temptation to eat the fruit of the forbidden tree. The moment she did, she committed sin. This act of rebellion was later copied by her husband, and so the first human pair precipitated a catastrophe that has had far greater repercussions than many realize.

Sin, which at its root is an attempt to control one's life and destiny apart from God, is a vile and heinous thing. So damaging was this original act of rebellion, that it upset the balance of the universe. Now why God didn't just sweep the whole mess aside and start again, we will never fully understand until we get to heaven.

One answer might be that he wanted to use the opportunity to demonstrate not just his power, but his wisdom and his grace. To eliminate man at that stage would show how powerful he was, but working through the disastrous situation and patiently introducing a plan that would one day involve his own Son's death on a cross, brought out an aspect of his character that otherwise the universe might never have known.

Some have wondered why God should have made the

material creation and Adam and Eve's posterity suffer for what, after all, was the sin of just two individuals. There is a theological explanation for that, far too complicated, I am afraid, to go into here. Suffice it to say that for good reasons God balanced the ages on the decision of that first human pair. They could have taken the universe through into continued peace and harmony or they could bring about its dissolution and ruin.

Their sin, as we well know to our cost, introduced into the universe a cataclysmic disturbance that threw it off-balance, with the result that the whole of creation, including man, became subject to decay, death, sickness and disease.

Everything that lives is subject to sickness and disease—whether human beings, animals or plants. All life is strangely poisoned at the fount.

Dr W. E. Sangster tells how once when travelling through Egypt he stood and watched a herd of water buffalo. Someone in the party remarked that the buffalo was the only animal not subject to disease. It died, said the man, only of old age. When Dr Sangster returned to this country, he contacted a friend of his, a zoologist, and asked if that statement was true. 'Nonsense,' said the zoologist. 'It's a hardy animal, of that there's no doubt, but like every other living thing in this universe, it does not escape the malady of sickness and disease.'

The sin of Adam and Eve was responsible for the whole of creation becoming subject to the evils of which we are speaking. Death, decay, disease, genetic failure, glandular disturbances, and all other types of physical malfunction sprang directly from this original transgression.

The apostle Paul, inspired by the Holy Spirit, wrote: 'We know that the whole creation has been groaning in travail....and not only the creation, but we ourselves...groan inwardly as we wait for adoption...the redemption of our bodies' (Rom 8:22–23, RSV).

That groan is the protest of a creation that was designed for better things. Sickness and disease is an intruder in God's universe, and it began, not by the will of the Almighty, but by the rebellion of the first human pair, who chose to establish their independence in a universe that God had created for himself as well as them.

Although this explains where sickness and disease come from, it does not answer all the problems concerning the subject. We have to look still further if we want an answer to the question we posed at the beginning of this chapter: Why do we become ill?

2. Sickness and disease come upon us because of our failure to obey the laws of health and healing that God has built into the universe

We saw in the previous chapter that God has built into the universe a law of health, and, like all laws, if we are to benefit from it, we have to obey it.

A strange thing happened in one of our British courts several years ago. A man was charged with having a television set without a licence. He pleaded that the set was not really his, that he had received it from the dealer on approval. He had not decided to buy it, and until he came to a decision, he felt that he was under no obligation to take out a licence.

The judge fined him. 'The law knows nothing about approval,' he said. 'The law is to be obeyed. Pay the fine!'

God's law are the same. They are not placed there on approval. They are there to be obeyed. And that is not because of capriciousness on the part of the Almighty. God is not a despotic tyrant who delights in throwing his weight around. He has built his laws into the universe (moral as well as physical) for the *benefit* of mankind. When we obey them, as we said, we get the rewards: when we violate them, we must suffer the consequences.

Some view the presence of laws in the universe as irksome and restricting. They adopt a take-it-or-leave-it attitude to such things. One writer, commenting on this attitude, says, 'If you are thinking of buying a garment, you can take it or leave it. If you are thinking of buying a house, you can take it or leave it. If you are thinking about buying a car, you can take it or leave it. But when you are thinking about the laws which God has established in the universe for mankind's benefit, you can only take them. If you break them, they will ultimately break you.'

God's laws are impersonal. The laws that God has built into his universe, including the law of health and healing, are quite impersonal. They have no feelings about us, one way or the other. Laws can't think. Neither do they make judgements. If we obey them, they benefit us. If we disobey them, they punish us.

Recently I read a report of a mother who had lost her child in a tragic accident. She was bathing her three-year-old son in the bathroom, which that particular morning seemed extremely cold. Going into the living-room, she unplugged an electric fire and installed it in the bathroom. Knowing it was a dangerous thing to do, she kept it well away from the bath, but at that moment the telephone rang and she went to answer it.

While she was out of the bathroom, a period of not more than a minute or so, her son, obviously feeling the cold, got out of the bath, picked up the fire and balanced it on the edge of the bath. When he got back into the bath, he accidentally knocked the fire into the water. He was instantly electrocuted and died.

The mother, as you can imagine, was deeply distraught. In an interview with a local reporter, she said, 'If there is a God, how could he let such a thing happen?'

We can understand the woman's dilemma, of course, and feel a deep sympathy for her, but *it was not God's fault*. To blame God for that is like blaming Henry Ford for all the automobile accidents that take place.

Laws do what they are supposed to do. They cannot make allowances for our mistakes. This may seem cruel at times, but natural and physical laws *must* punish us when we violate them.

'What law is to blame,' asks C. S. Lovett, 'when someone leaves a gate open to a swimming pool and a little toddler is drowned? God's law of physics says no one can live with his lungs full of water. Co-operating with that law would have saved the child's life. It is man's responsibility to acquaint himself with God's laws, especially those which have to do with health and survival.'

What happens when we decide to ignore God's laws? As free agents we can, of course, decide to ignore God's laws. But what happens when we do? We suffer the consequences.

One of the laws of survival and health is that the body needs physical exercise in order to stay in shape and function effectively. What happens if we ignore that and lie still for weeks or months without moving a single limb or muscle? The body will develop all kinds of problems from sores to cirhossis. Our bodies were made for movement, and if they don't get that then they protest, give up on us, and atrophy.

The same thing can be said about another of the laws of health: that we must eat a balanced diet if we are to maintain a good, sound constitution. If we live on a diet of junk food then, in due course, the body is going to object. It will say, in effect, 'I was not designed for this kind of treatment,' and will begin to malfunction.

Not long ago my wife and I took our grandchildren to Windsor Safari Park to see the animals. The people who run it take great care of the livestock. Everywhere there were signs that said: 'Do not feed the animals.' This is because the owners prepare special meals for them and control their diet so that they get the right food, which helps to ensure that they live good, long and healthy lives.

Given a proper diet, animals stay healthy and fit and don't become ill. It's the same with humans. If we fail to obey the laws that govern and regulate our health, then we must suffer the consequences. And the consequences of disobedience are sometimes fatal.

How seriously must we abide by God's dietary laws? A question I am often asked whenever the subject of health and healing is discussed is this: 'Are we as Christian believers under an obligation to keep to the dietary laws given by God to Moses in the Old Testament?'

Before answering that question, let's take a brief look at some of the laws that directly relate to health in the Old Testament. These laws were first given in approximately 1445 BC when God issued about twenty-five commands to the people of Israel in the Sinai desert. The commands are recorded primarily in Leviticus, chapters 11 to 15, and Deuteronomy 14.

God gave his people instructions on what food should be eaten. In Leviticus 11:1–8, God told Moses which animals were 'clean' and could be eaten. Among livestock, only those with cloven hooves that chew the cud were clean. Thus cows, sheep, goats and deer were acceptable (Deut 14:4). Non-cud eaters, such as the pig and pawed animals, were forbidden, including the rabbit, the mouse and the rat.

From the seas and streams, whatever had fins and scales could be eaten, but shellfish were taboo. Specific birds were forbidden including the vulture and the buzzard.

The people of Israel were also forbidden to eat anything that had died a natural death (Deut 14:21). The blood of the animal was also not to be eaten (Deut 12:16).

There were no rules governing fruit and vegetables, for these had been allowed since the beginning of creation (Gen 1:29).

What place should these Old Testament regulations have today?

I do not believe we are under a *legal* obligation to keep these dietary laws, although there is good evidence to show that there are physical benefits to be had from following many, if not all, of them.

For instance, with today's refrigeration devices, there is no need to throw away meat on the third day after slaughter, as did the ancient Israelites. Inspection of pigs and thorough cooking of pork virtually eliminates risk of trichinosis. Shellfish, harvested away from harbours where wastes are deposited, are fairly free of disease. Where risks exist, every effort should be made to avoid them, but our approach should be one of flexibility, based on knowledge, rather than on a fearful legalism.

My personal inclination is to keep to these dietary laws as much as possible. I avoid shellfish, and keep away from blood and fatty meats, such as pork, in order to reduce the risk of arteriosclerosis. But there are occasions, such as when I am staying in someone's home, where I will eat some of those things without question. I value highly the dietary laws of the Old Testament, but I do not approach them with a legalistic attitude, but with one of understanding.

The Old Testament health regulations have tremendous value and, when knowledgeably applied, lead to immense physical benefits. While we, under grace, are under no obligation to the law, we should appreciate that the Mosaic health practices anticipated modern medical discoveries and, where there is doubt, one ought to err in the direction of God's ancient order.

A Christian should make every effort to abide by the laws that govern health. This means making sure one gets enough sleep, eats a balanced diet, engages in a certain amount of physical activity each day, tries to avoid becoming overweight, and tries to avoid any contact with infectious diseases.

In relation to the laws that govern our health, it is not a matter of give and take. There is no give or take. When we disregard these laws, we do so to our peril.

3. *Sickness and disease come upon us as a result of mental and emotional stress*

Dr Hans Selye, a Canadian research scientist, believes that most of the chemical imbalance that occurs in the body is due to stress. 'If future events prove this concept correct,' states the *Journal of the American Medical Association*, 'it will be one of the most significant medical advances of this century.'

The way we respond to stress, according to Selye's theory, is governed mainly by three tiny glands: the pituitary, which nestles under the brain, and the two adrenals, which sit on top of the kidneys. All of them together weigh only about a third of an ounce, yet their potent hormones combat stress and fight off any threat to the body's welfare.

In today's world, says Selye, we allow ourselves to be subjected to too many stresses. We hurry constantly and we worry incessantly. The businessman drives himself all day and then spends most of the night worrying. The average housewife has so many pressures to face that it's no wonder that she can't get to sleep without a sleeping pill.

Our glands attempt to adjust to the constant demands of stress, pouring out the hormones the body needs to keep going. But as such a lifestyle is opposed to the way God designed us to live, the defence system of the body eventually breaks down itself.

Arteries harden, blood pressure rises, heart disease develops and arthritis strikes. 'The *apparent* cause of illness,' says Selye, 'is often an infection, nervous exhaustion or merely old age. But actually a breakdown of the hormonal-adaptation mechanisms appears to be the most common ultimate cause of death.'

As a medical student, Hans Selye noticed that his tutors used to talk a great deal about specific diseases with specific causes, such as pneumonia and the microbe that caused it.

'What about non-specific diseases?' Selye kept asking. 'What about the *feeling* of being sick?'

At first they laughed at him, but over the years, backed up by experiments, he has come to be regarded as one of the great medical prophets of the twentieth century. Because of his experiments, in which he has shown that stress is a prime factor in the development of sickness and disease, he has ensured for himself a place in medical history.

Doctors, who at one time were solely concerned with bacteria and infection, are now beginning to see that the mind can trigger off many physical problems. The popular term used to describe disorders that originate in the mind is psychosomatic. It comes from two Greek words: *psyche* (soul) and *soma* (body).

Dr S. I. McMillen, in his book *None of These Diseases*, presents a list of disorders caused or aggravated by mental and emotional stress. His list covers almost two pages. Significant among them are these:

ulcers
rheumatic fever
constipation
urological problems
diarrhoea
headaches
high blood pressure
epilepsy
arteriosclerosis
diabetes
coronary thrombosis
nervous disorders
hay fever and allergies
infections
backaches and muscular pain
eye and skin diseases

Some would add cancer to the list. In relation to this, one book that has intrigued me is *Mind as Healer, Mind as Slayer* by Kenneth R. Pelletier, professor of psychology at the University of California. According to Pelletier, *all* disorders are psychosomatic, in the sense that mind and body are involved in their aetiology (origination).

Any disorder, he claims, is created out of a complex interaction of social factors, physical and psychological stress, the personality of the person subjected to these influences and the inability of the person to adapt adequately to pressures.

Once sickness or illness is viewed in this way (as a complex interaction of many factors), then it is possible, he claims, to see symptoms as an early indication of excessive strain upon the mind-body system.

'A medical symptom,' Pelletier observes, 'may be a useful signal of the need for change in other parts of the person's life.' Other doctors such as Lawrence LeShan, a psychologist and author of *You Can Fight For Your Life*, have suggested that 'cancer patients were generally depressed *before* becoming ill, and that psychological issues were part of the aetiology of their illness.'

Some medical specialists believe in the existence of a cancer-prone personality, or a link between traumatic life events and the development of tumours, heart disease or other serious physical maladies.

What, according to these thinkers, are the ingredients that go to make up a cancer-prone personality?

He is a person who:

has characteristic facial tensions (squinting, grinding of teeth, etc.);
wills people to talk faster;
engages in frequent expiratory sighs;
uses four-letter words frequently;
clenches fists when upset;
is impatient;
thinks about doing two or more things at the same time;
eats meals too quickly;
has difficulty in doing nothing;
is easily irritated by others;
tends to hold resentments and is unable to forgive;
is prone to self-pity;
is bad at making relationships;
has a poor self-image;
is obsessed with success at any cost.

This kind of person is known to psychologists as engaging in what they call Type A behaviour. Type A temperaments are predisposed towards the more serious diseases such as cancer, heart disease and so on.

In fact, one of the breakthroughs in the field of cancer medicine is that made by Dr O. Carl Simonton, a Texas doctor, who is convinced that psychological forces play an important role in the development of cancer, and that those same forces can be mobilized to defeat or delay its course.

In his opinion, cancer flourishes in an atmosphere of mental or emotional despair, and one of the most effective ways of combating the disease is a special technique he has developed called 'imaging'. In this process, patients conjure up mental images of a sort of battlefield on which healthy cells are observed as putting the malignant ones to flight. A number of people claim to have been cured of cancer by this method. (For a fuller explanation of 'imaging', read *Getting Well Again* by O. Carl and Stephanie Simonton, published by Bantam Books.)

Many doctors are becoming convinced that there is an important interrelation between mind and body, and that this connection ought to be taken more seriously. The Bible, of course, has recognized this relationship between mind and body from the beginning of time.

As far back as the Old Testament, the connection between the mind and the body was known. Take just one example, 'Amnon was so upset by his passion for his sister Tamar, that it made him ill' (2 Sam 13:2, MOFFATT). Amnon's thoughts of having sex with his sister set up such an internal conflict within him that it made him ill. His attitudes were sick, and soon his body became sick.

When God made us in the beginning, he made us in such a way that the body and mind are intertwined. In fact, perhaps we should say body-mind rather than body and mind. One doctor says: 'A bodily disease that we look upon as whole and entire in itself, may, after all, be a symptom of some ailment or stress in the mind.' How true.

There are still some, of course, who say that all sickness and disease has a physical origin—they are the materialists. There are others who say that all disease has a mental or spiritual origin—they are the mentalists. To hold either position is to fly in the face of the facts. Both positions have led people to an early grave as a result of their half-truths.

Some sicknesses have a purely physical origin, and some have a mental origin. We must be open to all possibilities if we are to understand this subject correctly. The truth in each point of view has been established: the error in each should be eliminated.

Fred Stansberry, Stewardship Director for *Evangelical Ministries,* says that the word of God encourages us to take as much care of our minds as it does of our bodies.

One of these laws can be seen in Romans 12: 'Don't let the world around you squeeze you into its own mould, but let God re-make you so that your whole attitude of mind is changed' (v.2, PHILLIPS). Another is in Philippians 4: 'Fix your minds on whatever is true and honourable and just and pure and lovely and admirable' (v.8, PHILLIPS).

To summarize what I have said in this chapter: sickness comes from three main causes. One is as the result of physical impairment and malfunctioning owing to the Fall. Adam and Eve, through their original sin, opened up the universe to dissolution and decay. As a result of this, our physical beings are open to such things as genetic failures, hereditary traits, etc., which are passed on from one generation to another.

A second cause for sickness is when we violate the laws of health. A person can exhaust his body through overwork. He can chill it by exposure to the elements. He can overfeed it, get it too hot or too wet for a long time. He can let it deteriorate through inattention to exercise. Or he can poison it by eating the wrong foods.

A third cause for sickness is mental and emotional

stress. The mind can make us sick. People can actually think themselves into hospital. And, if some medical experts are to be believed, three out of four people who fill our hospital beds are there because their minds put them there.

Some Christians might wonder why I haven't included Satan as being a direct cause of sickness. I do not believe (except in rare circumstances) that Satan is able to directly bring about sickness in a human being. However, notwithstanding this, Satan is greatly involved in precipitating us towards sickness and disease, and precisely how he goes about this merits the treatment of a whole chapter.

5   Satan's Role in Sickness

How much influence does Satan have in the life of a Christian to bring about sickness, infirmity and disease? Quite a lot, I believe, but his influence is largely determined by the degree to which we permit him to operate in our lives.

Many Christians, as C. S. Lewis observed, fall into two equally opposite errors concerning the activity of Satan. They either overestimate him or they underestimate him. They regard him as having nothing to do with the occurrence of sickness or everything to do with it. The truth lies somewhere in the middle.

The Bible shows us that Satan is the arch-enemy of the human race who seeks, in every way he can, to disrupt and destroy the creation that God designed. In the world there are two kings and two kingdoms—the kingdom of God and the kingdom of Satan. And once we become Christians, we are thrust into the conflict between God and Satan, and commanded to fight.

Being saved doesn't mean being safe. As Christians we become the target of Satan's hatred and contempt, and he seeks in every way he can to disable us in the fight. We are not left to our own devices, however. God has provided us with protective armour which consists of a helmet of salvation, a breastplate of righteousness, a shield of faith, shoes of peace, the belt of truth, and the sword of the Spirit. This armour gives us complete protection against Satan and his forces (Eph 6:11–18).

Does Satan inflict us physically?

The question is often asked by Christians as to whether or not Satan has the power to bring about physical affliction or infirmity in a person's body. My own answer to that question is that although he may have the power to do it, generally he is not permitted to do so.

In the case of Job, Satan was permitted by God to afflict him with sickness and disease. This, I see, however, as an exception. There is, I believe, a hedge of protection placed around humanity, which is part of God's providential dealings towards his creation, and which restrains Satan from direct involvement with the human physiology.

If it were not for this providential arrangement, then, in my view, Satan would have annihilated the human race before now, and brought about its complete destruction.

This 'hedge of protection', which surrounds every human being, is part of our loving Creator's design to safeguard the human race from Satanic possession and oppression. If it were not there, then there is no doubt in my mind that I would not be writing these lines, and you would not be reading them.

There are times, however, when human beings, through occult involvement, provide Satan with an opportunity to penetrate that barrier, and in such cases it is possible for him to have direct access to the physiological functioning of that person.

About fifteen years ago, when I was pastoring a church

in central London, I spoke to a man who had been brought up in a home where each night his family had held an occult ritual, when the presence of Satan was invited.

He told me that, after a while, each member of the family developed a sickness that their doctor was unable either to diagnose or cure. The sickness, which took the form of a rash that completely covered their body from head to foot, resisted every kind of medication and treatment.

The strange thing was that the rash would completely disappear at the nightly rituals. 'It was as if,' the man told me, 'Satan was showing us the power he had in our lives by making the rash disappear and then return.' The family came to believe that the rash was the 'mark' of Satan's ownership of their lives, and they gradually came to accept it and live with it.

It was only when my friend became a Christian that he was able to disentangle himself from the influence of Satan in his life, but it was a number of months before the rash finally disappeared. I have known of several other cases where direct involvement with Satan has produced strange sicknesses or physical disabilities. But it is my conviction that such infirmities could not occur in the ordinary course of events, were it not for the handing over of direct control to Satan.

How does Satan work to bring about affliction?

If Satan is unable to have direct access to our physical frame, then how does he produce sickness and disease? He does it largely by involvement in our thought life. The *mind* is Satan's greatest battlefield. Listen to what the Scripture says concerning this:

But I fear, lest by any means, as the serpent beguiled Eve through his subtilty, so your minds should be corrupted from the simplicity that is in Christ (2 Cor 11:3, AV).

Again:

The weapons of our warfare are not carnal, but mighty through God to the pulling down of strong holds.... Casting down imaginations, and every high thing that exalteth itself against the knowledge of God, and bringing into captivity every thought to the obedience of Christ (2 Cor 10:4–5, AV).

The Bible has a good deal to say about the mind and about our thought life. The words 'think', 'thought' and 'mind' are used hundreds of times in the Scriptures. And what and how we think determines largely the way we feel—for good or bad. 'As he thinketh in his heart,' says the writer of the Proverbs, 'so is he' (23:7, AV).

One of the most interesting things I think I have ever discovered is the relationship of thoughts to feelings, and how feelings can affect physiological functioning.

Take this, for example: some years ago I was speaking at the Hayes Conference Centre in Derbyshire to a group of several hundred people on how our thoughts affect our emotions. To illustrate the point I wanted to make, I arranged beforehand with a young lady that, at some stage in my talk, I would point to her and say: 'Are you afraid of mice?' She would then nod her head and say: 'I certainly am.' Then I would say: 'Well, there is one by your foot.' At which she would leap on to a chair and scream for all she was worth.

When the appropriate moment arrived, we played our parts well. However, at the point when she leapt on to her chair and screamed, a number of other ladies nearby did the same thing. One lady, in fact, ran out through a side door. The whole meeting erupted. I was unable to continue with my lecture for several minutes.

When I explained that it was a put-up job, that it was all done to illustrate the point I was making, you can imagine the reaction. Some thought I had overstepped the mark, others thought it irresponsible and mischievous, while others considered it quite funny.

However, I doubt whether anyone who was there that day will forget the point I was making, that our thoughts and ideas greatly affect the way we feel, and the way we feel affects, in turn, the way we act and the way our bodies function.

Once those who disliked mice were told that one was running around by their feet, they *believed* it and so acted accordingly. They didn't have to decide which emotion they were going to feel. Fear came automatically. That fear set their entire defence system into action.

Their heart began to beat faster, adrenalin flowed into their bloodstream, and their body prepared for flight. All this happened despite the fact that there was no mouse present. But you see, once the mind had accepted the information (in this case, wrong information), then it automatically set in motion the body's defence systems.

The power of a thought or an idea in bringing about changes in the emotions or in the physiological system is quite amazing.

Have you heard of the trick that schoolboys sometimes play when one of their schoolmates gets up before the class to make a speech? Well, some of them take a slice of lemon and begin sucking on it. The poor victim, seeing the lemon in their mouths, would, through the power of his own thoughts, identify with it, and the effect of those thoughts causes the saliva to flow so heavily in his mouth that he is unable to go on with his speech!

The effect of emotions on the body

God has made us so that the way we think affects the way we feel, and the way we feel affects our bodies and the way they function. William James, the great psychologist, said, 'The greatest revolution in my generation was the discovery that human beings, by changing their inner attitudes of mind, can alter the outer aspects of their lives.'

Just as wrong thoughts and wrong emotions can alter the outer aspects of one's life, so can right thinking and right emotions.

Someone has defined an emotion as 'a change in the thoughts which produces a sensible change in the body'. Note: 'a *sensible* change'—an outer manifestation: the body changes for good or ill with the impact of the thought and the emotion. The British Medical Association says that there is not a single cell of the body totally removed from the influence of mind and emotions.

So the attitudes of mind and emotions do not stay attitudes: they have definite physical effects. We turn pale with fear. We blush with embarrassment. We are livid with rage. We quiver with excitement. We say things like: 'I feel ill thinking about it.' We *do* feel ill—for the situation we face affects our thoughts, our thoughts affect our emotions and our emotions produce 'sensible changes' in the body.

Dr Leslie Weatherhead tells of an experiment he did on a girl who was very susceptible to hypnotism. He gathered a group of doctors, hypnotized the girl, and told her that he was touching her knee with a red-hot iron. Instead he touched her with a pencil. Then he bandaged her knee, and invited one of the group to seal the bandage. A few days later, the group met again and when the bandage was taken off, they discovered a blister with water in it on the girl's knee.

The subconscious mind had produced the blister out of that subconscious thinking. I do not want you to read into this an endorsement of hypnotism (although hypnotism is, in fact, quite a simple human mechanism).

God has designed us so that we do not have to believe everything we hear. With our minds we can evaluate, check, weigh and consider anything we are told, and then decide whether to accept or reject it. We can challenge people's assumptions, adopt an attitude of scepticism, or be suspicious. We can refuse to accept or believe what we hear unless we have a good reason for accepting it.

All a hypnotist does is to get us to relax the critical and evaluative processes of our conscious mind, and accept what he tells us as *fact*. Once we believe what he says, then the idea drops into our subconscious mind, where the automatic processes of our bodies take over. The brain instructs the body to carry out whatever function is demanded by the idea that has been given it. This may be an oversimplification of what takes place, but basically hypnotism follows those lines.

Once the mind grasps an idea, whether that idea be good or bad, the effect it has will be to bring about changes in the emotions and ultimately in the body.

A few years ago I read in an international magazine the story of a man who had a serious abdominal operation during which a small plastic window, the size of a half-penny, was built into his stomach.

For several months after the operation doctors were able to observe the contents of his stomach through this 'window'. They said that after a while they learned to tell the state of his thoughts and emotions by the appearance of his stomach lining.

When some papers, for which the man was responsible,

71

were lost and he thought he would lose his job, he became agitated, and the doctors noticed that the lining of his stomach got paler and paler. When the papers were found, his stomach returned to its normal pink colour. At one time, when he was reprimanded for something, he got red in the face, but dared not express his anger at the person concerned. This caused the gastric acid in his stomach to increase. A few days later, the doctors noticed small haemorrhages on the surface of the stomach lining.

The lesson is quite clear. Our thoughts affect our emotions which, in turn, affect our bodies. Wrong thoughts may not always result in sickness, but our bodies register them nevertheless, and we become predisposed to illness.

Ever heard of a phantom pregnancy? It happens much more than we may realize. A woman wants a baby so badly that she convinces herself that she is pregnant. Her body accepts the idea and goes along with it obligingly by producing all the signs of a pregnancy—distended abdomen and all. Under an anaesthetic, the abdomen flattens out to normal. When the thought pressure is removed by medical means, then the symptoms disappear.

What has this to do with Satan?

One of Satan's main strategies, as we have seen, is to wage war against our minds. The apostle Peter reminds us to be constantly on the alert:

> Be careful—watch out for attacks from Satan, your great enemy. He prowls around like a hungry, roaring lion, looking for some victim to tear apart. Stand firm when he attacks. Trust the Lord; and remember that other Christians all around the world are going through these sufferings too (1 Pet 5:8–9, TLB).

The way in which the personality has been constructed by God gives Satan an advantage through which he can operate. He can plant ideas in the mind that are not true, but if they are accepted by us as true, then the automatic functions of the body take over and make us ill. Satan can damage our bodies with false ideas.

And one of the avenues through which he best works is the imagination. Vincent Collins, in *Me, Myself and You*, says of the imagination:

> Imagination is to the emotions what illustrations are to a text, what music is to a ballad. It is the ability to form mental pictures, to visualise irritating or fearful situations in concrete form. As soon as we perceive a feeling and begin to think about it, the imagination goes to work. The imagination reinforces the thoughts, the thoughts intensify the feelings and the whole business builds up. There is only one way to beat this game and that is to stop the thoughts in their tracks and blot out the imaginary pictures. Fearful or angry feelings and thoughts generate pressure, and the pressure will continue to increase as long as the build-up process is allowed to continue.

Some speak disparagingly of the imagination. They place it in the same category as fancy or speculation. But imagination is one of God's greatest gifts to men. It's the ability to see something before it exists.

'Every great feat has to be *imagined* first in the mind,' says one writer, 'before it can be turned into reality.' Remember Alcock and Brown? They were the first to fly the Atlantic. They told a newspaper reporter that they had flown it a thousand times in their imagination before they flew it in reality. Indeed, it was probably essential to their success that they flew it first in their imagination or else they might never have flown it at all.

They had to see the vast expanse of water beneath

them. They had to visualize the banks of cloud, shutting out the view. They had to imagine the weather conditions, feel the cold, and try to anticipate the problems that might arise. And the difficulties they saw in their imagination, they prepared for in simple fact. The keener their imagination, the more complete their preparation.

One morning in June 1919, when surrounded by extreme peril, they knew what to do because they had already anticipated the problem. Yes, all great feats often start in the imagination, and imagination is one of God's greatest gifts to men.

But the same imagination that can sweep us towards success can plunge us into despair. Once Satan is permitted to tamper with its mechanisms, he can turn it to our disadvantage. And Satan is an expert at tampering with the imagination. You know something of that if you have spent a sleepless night, tossing and turning, because you feared the worst.

Fear soon follows in the wake of the pictures that are thrown up by the imagination. All Satan needs to do is drop a negative picture into our imagination and the mechanisms of our personality take it from there.

How many times have you said to yourself: 'I'm worried sick over this thing?' Well, you are quite correct in putting worry and sickness together, but in fact your worry is probably needless. Most of the things we worry about never happen.

Even though Satan is able to feed negative and destructive thoughts into our minds, these suggestions, by themselves, cannot make us sick. It takes our consent and co-operation to do that. God has given us a free will by which we are able to choose what thoughts we are going to focus upon. The prophet Isaiah had this in mind when he wrote: 'Thou wilt keep him in perfect peace, whose mind is stayed on thee' (26:3). The margin note in the Authorized Version states: 'mind: thought or imagination'. The verse could quite justifiably be translated: 'Thou wilt keep him in perfect peace whose imagination stops at thee.'

We are not able to prevent Satan from influencing our thought life, but we are able to take over the control of our thoughts. We can decide precisely what thoughts we will allow to dominate our minds. We do not have to accept Satan's ideas, and once we understand this, we are on the way to achieving a great victory in our lives, for what we think, we are.

Control your thoughts and you are on the way to freedom from fear, worry, delusion *and* sickness.

6   *God's Many Delivery Systems*

'God,' said a famous Christian physician, 'is the source of all true healing, but he has many delivery systems. The secret is to discern which one is the right one for you.'

In this chapter we will look at the major ways through which God sends his healing power into our lives, so that we might be aware of the many avenues of healing that are available to us.

God heals through the laying on of hands

In Mark's Gospel, chapter 16, we read that 'they shall lay hands on the sick, and they shall recover' (v.18). Some think that the ministry of the 'laying on of hands' should only be practised in the context of evangelism, so that unbelievers might witness the miraculous power of Jesus Christ and be converted, but there is no scriptural warrant for believing this.

Many great and wonderful healings have taken place as believers have laid their hands on others and prayed that they might be healed.

On one occasion in the early 1960s, Sam Park, a Korean, came to my home through the most astonishing circumstances. He informed me that he was suffering from tuberculosis. Sam was a high school principal in Pusan, South Korea, and was in Europe on a special mission to various churches to make known the needs of his work.

One morning when in Zurich, he took a drink of water and immediately he began to cough up blood. Realizing that he was in a serious condition, and having suffered for some time with tuberculosis, he feared to go for medical treatment lest he be detained in Switzerland, unable to return home.

As he prayed, God drew my name to his attention, and through a series of remarkable events, he eventually found where I lived, and made his way to my home.

When I saw him he was in a desperate and distressed condition. He told me that he was bleeding from the lungs, but that if I would lay my hands upon him and pray, then he would be healed.

My initial reaction to what he said was to wish that God had led him to someone else. I felt inadequate to deal with his condition, and felt that I needed to spend two or three days in prayer and fasting before praying for such a desperate physical need.

Sam saw my consternation and said, 'Don't worry, just do what God says in his word and leave the rest to him. Lay your hands on me, as it says in Mark 16, and God will heal me.' I never laid hands more tremulously and tentatively on anyone in my whole life, but within minutes he was instantly and completely healed.

Later, after we had praised God together and given him thanks for the miracle he had performed, Sam said, 'I feel extremely hungry. I haven't eaten for several days. Is it possible for me to have something to eat, please?'

My wife, thinking that solid food would be inappropriate, suggested something light and milky. 'I think, if I may,' he said, 'some bacon and eggs.'

Bacon and eggs? I could hardly believe my ears! He had not eaten for days, and just minutes ago was coughing up blood. But such are the wonderful works of God.

Some months later, when I was conducting an evangelistic crusade in Sam's home town of Pusan in Korea, I invited him to give his testimony to the large crowd of 30,000 people who gathered there each night of the crusade. The impact his testimony made on that crowd was so great that hundreds, including a Buddhist priest, surrendered their lives to Christ.

The laying on of hands is one of God's ordained delivery systems that bring his healing power to men and women. Although God's other delivery systems were available to Sam, at that particular time the laying on of hands was *the* one for him.

God heals through anointing with oil and the prayer of faith

Another of God's delivery systems through which healing can come is the simple practice of anointing with oil and praying the prayer of faith.

James 5:14 says: 'Is any one of you sick? He should call the elders of the church to pray over him and anoint him with oil in the name of the Lord' (NIV).

Notice the words, '*He should call* the elders of the church.' It is quite clear from this that the person who is sick must initiate the action—he has to *call*. Canon Jim Glennon of St Andrew's Cathedral, Sydney, who is well known in Australia and other parts of the world for his healing ministry, says, 'I have found that whenever I have initiated the contact with someone in need, simply because he was in need, my prayer has seldom been effective. Indeed, so much so, that now I would not approach anyone and offer to pray the prayer of faith for his or her healing.'

This observation is in line with my own thinking and experience, for I have found that there is a degree of expectancy and faith in a person who asks for healing that is not found in the heart of someone who waits to be asked.

Why the use of oil? Anointing with oil is a symbol of the Holy Spirit (Acts 10:38). Instructions about the use of oil must have been given to the disciples, for they anointed with oil during our Lord's earthly ministry (Mk 6:13), but no explanation for the practice is recorded.

The kings of Israel were consecrated to their office by being anointed with oil (1 Sam 10:1, 2 Sam 2:4 and 5:3, 1 Kings 1:39). Priests were also consecrated in that way (Ex 29:7, 40:13–15, Lev 8:1–12).

God often uses physical things to reinforce spiritual truth, as, for example, water baptism and holy communion. In the same way, oil assists us to visualize spiritual reality. In the days when I was a pastor, I was frequently called upon, along with the elders of the church, to pray for those who were sick, anointing them with oil in the name of the Lord. Often, as I watched the oil slowly trickle on to a person's head, it generated faith in me.

I have never regarded the oil as having supernatural properties; I just know from experience that as it was poured out, the sight of it helped to stir my faith into fervent, believing, intercessory prayer.

We have answered the question 'why oil?' Now we turn to the question 'why elders?' The answer, I believe, is because elders should be men of faith, appointed by the Holy Spirit and able to feed the church of God

(Acts 20:28). In fact, all who held office in the early church were expected to be men of high standing, even those who waited on tables (Acts 6:3).

The elders of the church represent the whole body of believers and, as they pray, at the same time anointing the sick person with oil, they are drawing upon and focusing the faith of that local church into an act of healing.

The kind of praying the elders are to engage in, says James, is the prayer of faith. The question is often asked, 'What constitutes the prayer of faith?'

I remember speaking on this subject in a certain church, and I said something like this: 'The prayer of faith is based on two things, one, believing that God wants to heal the person concerned, and two, believing without doubt that God will answer.'

After the service two elders approached me and said, 'If what you have said is true then we feel disqualified from being elders in this church because, one, we are never sure that God *always* wants to heal, and two, we are never sure that our prayers are going to be answered. We pray with positive words, but they are nothing more than words. Our hearts are not really in it.'

I encouraged them to sit down and study the Scriptures together in an attempt to clarify their thinking on the willingness and eagerness of God to heal. I said, 'Once you see clearly, from the word of God, that the Almighty does not send sickness, and is fully committed to delivering his children from both sin and sickness, then your prayers will be full of divine confidence. You will pray the prayer of faith.'

I don't know what happened to those two elders, but the more I have to do with people in leadership positions in the church, the more concerned I become about their negative views in relation to the healing promises and power of the Lord Jesus Christ.

How can we pray the prayer of faith if we are uncertain as to whether or not God wants to heal the person upon whose head we place the anointing oil?

My own view of the church at this present time is that, in relation to this important passage in James 5:14, the anointing of oil has become for many (not all) a meaningless ritual.

God heals through holy communion

I am convinced that the Christian church, while aware of the spiritual healing to be found in the service of holy communion, has never fully understood its potential for securing release from physical afflictions and infirmities.

Listen once again to the well-known words of the apostle Paul in his letter to the Corinthians: 'For I have received of the Lord that which also I delivered to you, That the Lord Jesus the same night in which he was betrayed took bread: And when he had given thanks, he brake it, and said, Take, eat: this is *my body, which is broken for you*' (1 Cor 11:23–24, AV).

Let's focus for a moment on the broken bread, symbolic of our Lord's broken body. At the moment of communion, you take that piece of *broken* bread, place it in your mouth, at the same time remembering the brokenness of Christ upon the cross.

The moment it enters your mouth, your whole physical system is placed on the alert that something is about to enter the digestive system. You swallow it, and it passes into your stomach. You have received into your body a piece of bread that symbolizes the death of the Lord Jesus Christ. At such a moment, a fresh and vivid sense of Christ's atonement is impressed deeply into your spirit. I said before that God often uses physical things to

82

help us become aware of spiritual realities.

Taking the bread and eating it (a simple physical act) opens up the avenues of the spirit to comprehend and absorb the benefits of Christ's death, and through this your spiritual capacities are ministered to in a way that is deeply mysterious and beyond logical explanation.

Wonderful as this is, however, how more wonderful it would be if, when we are sick, we would open our beings to receive the healing might and power of our Lord Jesus Christ. There have been hundreds of occasions in my life, since discovering the healing potential in the communion service, when, tired, weary or sick, I have used the moment of taking and eating the bread as an opportunity of letting God's healing power flow into my body.

I say to myself, 'Lord, just as I receive this bread into my body so now, by an act of faith, I receive the broken bread of your healing power, which you won for me on Calvary, into the whole of my being. Thank you, Lord Jesus, I believe it is done.'

Following the receiving of the bread comes the drinking of the wine. The apostle Paul said of this: 'After the same manner also he took the cup, when he had supped, saying, This cup is the new testament in my blood: this do ye, as oft as ye drink it, in remembrance of me' (1 Cor 11:25, AV).

The significance of the wine is to remind us of Christ's blood which was shed for us on Calvary. Here again God uses a physical thing—blood—to remind us of a spiritual reality—redemption.

Although the primary purpose of the communion service is to make a *spiritual* impact upon our lives, it can also trigger our faith in relation to physical healing. Every communion service should be a divine healing service if Christians who are sick are present.

One of the greatest provisions for both spiritual and physical enrichment lies in the act of communion, but few seem to obtain from it all that God has put into it. It is my conviction that if Christians came to the Eucharist, or the Lord's Supper, fully appropriating its spiritual and physical benefits every Sunday, then they would not have to make their way so often to the doctor's surgery on a Monday.

God heals in response to petitionary or intercessory prayer

The Christian church, generally speaking, uses the terms petitionary prayer and intercessory prayer in this way: petitionary prayer is prayer on behalf of ourselves, and intercessory prayer is prayer on behalf of others.

There are thousands of Christians who, when they become ill, simply fall upon their knees and petition God to heal them—and he does. There are occasions, of course, when a person, suffering from a serious sickness, might find petitionary prayer difficult, if not impossible, but such occasions are more the exception than the rule.

There are many Scriptures that confirm the fact that it is right and proper to pray for ourselves whenever we have a need:

> Ask and it will be given to you; seek and you will find; knock and the door will be opened to you. For everyone who asks receives; he who seeks finds; and to him who knocks the door will be opened (Lk 11:9–10, NIV).

The apostle James reminds us that one of the reasons why we do not receive many more blessings from God is simply because we do not ask: 'You do not have, because you do not ask God' (4:2, NIV).

There are some Christians who regard petitionary prayer with suspicion. They say that it tempts one

84

towards self-preoccupation. But, as Dr W. E. Sangster says, 'Some requests leap from the heart because they must. A man's child may be desperately ill, or the doctor may suspect a malignant growth in the man's wife...how can a believing man not help but pray? He would have to throttle himself to prevent the pleading words pouring from his lips—and God does not expect us to check ourselves in hours like these.'

Any theory of prayer that prevents a person going to God in an hour of great need must be condemned. The heart cries out against it.

Those who have some experience of the healing ministry are convinced of the importance and power of intercessory prayer. One of the things that fills me with hope as I survey the contemporary Christian scene here in the British Isles, is the news that in churches of all denominations small groups are being formed for the purpose of bringing the urgent needs of fellow Christians before God in intercessory prayer.

These small groups, sometimes just two or three people, are acting in accordance with the promise of our Lord who said, 'If two of you on earth agree about anything you ask for, it will be done for you by my Father in heaven. For where two or three come together in my name, there am I with them' (Mt 18:19–20, NIV).

Recently I asked a leader of such a group: 'Intercessory prayer is hard and intensive work; how do you go about the task of bringing people before God in prayer?' His reply was so illuminating that I thought I would quote it here verbatim:

Whenever a person is brought before us with a need, we visualize that person in our minds as clearly as we can. We *think* of them. See them! See them in their sick or distressed condition. We do not dwell too much on their sickness nor try to 'feel' as they do. That would sabotage our effectiveness in building up a positive prayer approach. We think of them as they can be in God—well and whole.

Next we focus our thoughts upon God. We think of his power, his goodness, his grace, his might, and when we have a clear picture in our minds of the sick one and of God we bring them *together* in the crucible of our believing hearts. We hold them there together as long as we can. We don't spend too much time particularizing our request (it is known anyway to God), but we concentrate more on becoming the channel between him and the needy person. Our ministry is to be a channel between his heart and theirs.

Prayer reaches out to avail itself of all the resources of God. Intercessory prayer is a conduit through which God's power passes into the hearts and lives of the needy and the distressed. The church has yet to see the marvels and miracles that can be wrought through sacrificial, concentrated, widespread intercessory prayer.

God heals through doctors and medicines

Someone has said, 'Religion and medicine need each other. If we had to rely on our weak human faith alone, how many of us would be alive today?'

Christians in general have contradictory attitudes towards the medical profession. Some have little faith in God's willingness to heal through supernatural means, but have a great deal of faith in the efforts and skill of their local GP. Others have little or no respect for the medical profession, and put their trust solely and entirely in God. If God does not bring about their healing through direct spiritual means, they feel it right to live with their problem or consult a doctor only as a last resort.

Some time ago I came across a quotation from the book of Sirach, an ancient document dated around the second century BC when medicine was in its infancy. This is what it said:

> Hold the physician in honour for he is essential
>   to you, and God who established his profession.
> From God, the doctor has his wisdom, and the king provides
>   for his sustenance.
> His knowledge makes the doctor distinguished and gives
>   him access to those in authority.
> God makes the earth yield healing herbs which the
>   prudent man should not neglect;
> Was not the water sweetened by a twig that men might
>   learn his power?
> He endows men with the knowledge to glory in his
>   mighty works
> Through which the doctor eases pain and the druggist
>   prepares his medicines.
> Thus God's creative work continues without cease in its
>   efficacy on the surface of the earth.
> My son, when you are ill, delay not, but pray to God
>   who will heal you:
> Flee wickedness, let your hands be just, cleanse your
>   heart of every sin:
> Offer your sweet smelling oblation and petition, a rich
>   offering according to your means.
> Then give the doctor his place lest he leave:
>   for you need him too.
> There are times that give him an advantage and he too
>   beseeches God
> That his diagnosis may be correct and his treatment
>   bring about a cure.
> He who is a sinner toward his Maker will be defiant
>   toward the doctor (Sir 38:1–15).

As a Christian I thank God for the work of doctors and all who are involved in the medical profession. In the first centuries AD, the Christian churches were centres of healing where sufferers came or were brought in order that they might be healed. One might say that the churches were the first hospitals.

However, after the Emperor Constantine was converted, Christianity became the accepted religion, and people came into the church, not through a genuine conversion, but because it was the fashionable thing to do. As a result, the church became weak and ineffective, filled with nominal Christians who knew little or nothing about the power of God.

As the miraculous element received less and less emphasis, people began to look more to man than to God. Humanism began to develop, until finally the idea of a compartmentalized life took the place of a unified life. Man's body was treated as if it were an end in itself rather than as an integral part of the soul and spirit.

Despite this, however, the first doctors to set foot in what is now the Third World were Christian missionary doctors who were supported by their fellow believers back home. Many believe that the medical missionary helped to bridge the gap between religion and medicine.

It is surely right that the church and medicine work hand in hand. The church should support and pray for all those who are engaged in the work of healing through medicine. We may not agree with all the methods used, but we ought to pray that every doctor, nurse and medical student might realize that they are the extensions of God's healing power.

Acceptance of the work of the medical profession does not in any way deny the reality of the supernatural side of healing. God can work miracles today as he has done throughout the past. We should expect him to do so, and invite him to do so much more than we are at present. Yet with all this we ought to keep in mind the wise words of Dr Martyn Lloyd-Jones when addressing the annual conference of the Christian Medical Fellowship at Bournemouth in 1971:

> God's *customary* way of dealing with diseases is through the
> therapeutic abilities he has given to men, and the drugs that
> he has put in such profusion in nature. But we are still to
> believe that with God 'all things are possible'.

7 Lord, Heal Me Now!

If, as we have seen, God is both eager and willing to heal us whenever we become ill, how do we go about the task of actually obtaining that healing?

In this chapter I want to give you ten simple but positive steps by which you can approach this important issue. These steps, I believe, are in harmony with Scripture, and bring together some of the concepts and insights that were advanced in the earlier chapters.

Studies show that, generally speaking, people respond in one of two ways whenever sickness or disease invades their lives. They either adopt a passive 'grin and bear it' attitude, or attempt to fight it with all the passion they can muster.

One doctor told me that medical people speak of a 'classic' cancer type—the quiet, accepting 'make no waves' person. We saw earlier that there is a type A personality which is prone to cancer, but it is also true that those with an attitude of passive acceptance—'This is the way it is—there is little that can be done about it'—can become prone to a serious sickness, such as cancer, too.

1. Remind yourself that since God wills your health, you should will it too

Be convinced of this—when you *will* health, you are not working against God but with him. You are in line with creation's purpose. Any doubt over this issue will sabotage your efforts to be made whole, so soak your mind in the Scriptures that show healing to be the Father's will for his children.

Here are some of them:

'Bless the Lord, O my soul, and forget not all his benefits: Who forgiveth all thine iniquities; who healeth all thy diseases' (Ps 103:2–3, AV).

'Is there no balm in Gilead; is there no physician there? why then is not the health of the daughter of my people recovered?' (Jer 8:22, AV).

'And he put forth his hand, and touched him, saying, I will: be thou clean. And immediately the leprosy departed from him' (Lk 5:13, AV).

'Heal me, O Lord, and I shall be healed; save me, and I shall be saved: for thou art my praise' (Jer 17:14, AV).

'Now when the sun was setting, all they that had any sick with divers diseases brought them unto him; and he laid his hands on every one of them, and healed them' (Lk 4:40, AV).

God does not will sickness and disease. They are intrusions into his universe. It is his *will* to heal you. Make it your will also.

2. *Obtain medical advice on the nature of your illness*

Sickness or disease (as we have seen) can come upon us for a number of different reasons, so get a thorough medical examination, then you will know whether the trouble is purely physical or whether it might be rooted in the mental or emotional part of your being.

If possible, consult a doctor who understands the relationship between mind and body. The materialist, one who sees disease as purely physical in its origin, is as out of date in today's advanced medicine as the Chinese medicine man who punctured his patients in order to let the devils out!

If an examination shows that the sickness is physiological, and an obvious remedy is available, then don't be afraid of letting God heal you through medication, or, if necessary, through surgery.

You will need to exercise caution over some forms of medication (such as strong drugs), but don't try to be more spiritual than God who has planted in nature the remedies for many of our diseases.

And don't, I beg you, think that because you have sought the advice of a doctor you have forfeited your right to be healed supernaturally by the Lord. Some Christians I know are afraid of receiving medical attention because they think that God will interpret their action as lack of faith.

Such people carry in their hearts a concept of God that is thoroughly unscriptural. God is a loving heavenly Father with a *Father's* love for his children. Those of you who are parents—would you treat *your* children with such disregard? Of course not. So stop thinking of God in this way. God can use the skill of the doctor to heal you or he can heal you directly through supernatural means. But don't think that the one is contradictory to the other.

3. *Go over your mental and spiritual attitudes and try to ascertain if they may be contributing to your sickness*

It is important to keep in mind that few illnesses or diseases are *purely* physical. God has designed us in such a way that the three parts of our being—spirit, soul and body—interact with each other. Our thoughts and attitudes can greatly affect our physiological functioning, and it is important to keep in mind that our attitudes as well as our arteries may need close inspection.

I have found, through long experience in counselling Christians, that there are four major attitudes that contribute to ill health. Someone called them 'The Fearsome Foursome'.

The first is *fear*. If there is fear in your life, it will upset your physiological functioning.

A young man told me that he was plagued with constant headaches for which his doctor could find no physiological reason. I encouraged him to examine his attitudes. When he did, he discovered that he was greatly defensive about the Christian faith. He argued it with everyone he met, and when someone came up with an argument that he couldn't counter, he became agitated and anxious. I suggested to him that he was operating from a position of fear, not faith. 'God's word,' I said, 'can defend itself. The fact that you can't answer all the arguments makes no difference to the truth of God's word.' He saw the point, surrendered his fear of being caught out, and his headaches disappeared.

The second major enemy of health is *resentment*. Dr Flanders Dunbar tells of a diabetic woman who suffered for seven years with severe pains that brought her to the verge of suicide. In talking with her doctor, she confessed that resentment and bitterness caused her more physical difficulties than potatoes, sweets or ice-cream. When she gave up her resentments, she obtained immediate relief from her pains.

Resentment is not only a poison in the mind, it produces poisons in the body too. Get rid of resentment—fast. It is an enemy of health.

The third is *guilt*. If the body is to be at its best then the soul and spirit must be free of haunting guilt. Guilt and health are incompatible—the two just don't fit together.

94

King David in Psalm 32 explains some of the physical problems he had to face when he clung to unconfessed guilt. 'There was a time when I wouldn't admit what a sinner I was,' he said. 'But my dishonesty made me miserable and filled my days with frustration.... My strength evaporated like water on a sunny day' (vv.3–4, TLB).

I am not talking here about false guilt, but *real* guilt. Some guilts are false, and deserve to be thrown overboard, so to speak, but real guilt, that is guilt that comes from violating a clear scriptural principle, must be dealt with by honest confession, and, where appropriate, restitution.

The fourth enemy of health is *self-centredness*. This means being overly self-concerned and self-preoccupied. Quite simply, God did not design you to function with *self* at the centre of your personality. He made you to be a God-centred individual, and unless your ego is marginal and God central then you won't function effectively.

Dr Adler, the famous psychiatrist, said, 'I suppose all the ills of human personality can be traced back to one thing; namely, not understanding the meaning of the statement, "It is more blessed to give than to receive."' Life that is turned outward to others is contributive. Life that is turned inward on oneself is cancerous.

Are any of these 'Fearsome Foursome', or any other wrong attitudes, at work in your life? Then get rid of them—right away—for they can reach out and poison your very nerves and tissues with disease.

4. *Acquaint yourself with the reasons why people are not healed so that you can prepare in advance to overcome them*

A great deal of research has been conducted in recent years by Christian doctors and ministers who have set out to answer the question: why are some people healed and others not? A lot of information has been gleaned as a result of this research, the more salient of which I want to present to you now in summarized form—as being aware of the reasons why some fail to be healed may help you.

(a) *Lack of faith*. Faith is one of the simplest yet at the same time one of the most complex of biblical subjects. Look at this verse, for example: 'So I tell you, whatever you pray for and ask, believe you have got it, and you shall have it' (Mk 11:24, MOFFATT). How can one believe that one already has health when sickness is perhaps so evident and rampant?

Faith is resting confidently on the fact that God is true to his word (Heb 11:1). Naturally speaking, we expect to see health before we believe we have it. Faith is believing we have it before we see it. And such faith can only come as we stand firmly on what God says in his word about his willingness to heal. As 'faith cometh by hearing, and hearing by the word of God' (Rom 10:17, AV), the more we read and study the word, the more effectively our faith will work for us whenever it is needed.

(b) *A wrong diagnosis*. Sometimes a doctor may make a wrong diagnosis and so prescribe the wrong treatment. It is possible, too, when attempting to discover the cause of our own sickness by self-diagnosis, that we can come to the wrong conclusions.

Just recently a man told me that he had borne an affliction for years owing, he thought, to a severe trauma he went through as a child. He discussed the matter with a Christian counsellor who was shown by the Lord that the physical problem he had was due, not so much to the trauma, but to the resentment he held towards his parents, who were partly responsible for the horror he had gone through.

96

The counsellor showed him that the Lord had already healed the hurt, but there was nothing he could do about the bitterness as long as he chose to retain it. When this was shown him, the man confessed his bitterness at once, and within days the physical problem he had borne for so long disappeared.

Because of our human frailty, we can easily become the victims of wrong diagnosis, whether by a doctor, ourselves or an experienced Christian.

A few years ago, a lady wrote to me saying that she was praying for her hyperactive child to be delivered from demonic influences. When I asked her how she knew the hyperactivity was due to demonic influence, she said that a minister had diagnosed it as such. I encouraged her to take the child to a specialist who diagnosed brain damage. Treatment was given, and the child soon became normal. Wrong diagnosis may be a rare occurrence, but it does happen, and such a possibility must always be kept in mind.

(c) *A wrong concept of God.* Some people project the concept they have of their parents on to God. If their parents were harsh, punitive and judgemental, this can produce a basic deficiency in their personality. They subconsciously punish themselves in order to please their parents.

This conditioning, brought about through an unhappy parent–child relationship, can cause a block in a person's ability to receive the blessings of health. Such people feel they are undeserving of God's goodness, and can only live with themselves when they are struggling under the load of a debilitating sickness or illness. This subconscious resistance hinders them from accepting the healing provision of Christ.

(d) *Unconfessed sin.* It ought to be quite clear by now that a violation of a moral principle can have its repercussions, not only in our spirit and in our soul, but in our body also. A minister told me of a girl in his church who asked for the prayers of the fellowship in relation to a serious physical problem that had developed in her life.

As they prayed together, they were filled with a sense of great expectancy that something was about to happen. It did—but not in the way they supposed. One of the elders went to the girl and whispered quietly in her ear that God had shown him that the cause of her problem was a certain unconfessed sin that she was committing. The girl was indignant at first that her sin had been exposed (although to no one other than the elder), but eventually she broke down, confessed the sin to God, and complete healing came within hours.

(e) *Refusal to apply medical advice*. I have already made clear that I firmly believe that doctors and medicines are the instruments God *ordinarily* uses to bring about healing.

Some Christians, once they have been prayed for according to the instructions given in James 5:14 or by a group of intercessors, feel that they need no longer take the prescribed medication. I know a girl in South Wales who died of diabetes because some of her Christian friends encouraged her to stop taking the insulin as a sign of her faith.

You can be sure that if God heals a person of diabetes, they will certainly know it—and so will the person's doctor. Until the evidence that one has been healed is clear, it is right and proper, in my view, to continue taking medication. It is never a lack of faith to follow professionally given medical advice.

5. *Face the question as honestly as you can: do I really want to get well?*

You might respond to this question by saying, 'But

surely no one *wants* to be sick?' Well, strange as it may seem, some people, despite their conscious desire to get well, subconsciously *want* to be sick.

This problem is nowhere more clearly illustrated than in the story of the man lying by the Pool of Bethesda (Jn 5:1–15)—the Jewish 'Lourdes' of its day.

The story surrounding the Pool of Bethesda was this: occasionally an angel came and disturbed the water, and the first one to get into the pool after that mysterious happening would be healed.

One man who had lain by that pool for thirty-eight years was asked by Jesus, 'Do you want to get well?' (v.6, NIV.) At first it sounds like a strange question to ask of a man who had sat there for such a long time. But Jesus, knowing that the lack of desire to get well is often deeply embedded in the subconscious, sought to get him to face the reality of the situation with a challenging question.

Some people use their sicknesses, albeit unconsciously, to serve their self-interest. They use sickness to gain power over others, to opt out of responsibility, to avoid the challenge of relationships, and for many other reasons.

A girl went to her doctor and asked his advice about a large purple lump that had appeared on her forehead. The doctor examined her and said that the lump had no physical origin, but was the result of some concern or worry in her life.

The girl faced her concerns, and within a few hours the lump had disappeared. The next day, however, the girl went once again to her doctor, this time complaining of cramping stomach pains. The doctor once again diagnosed that there was no physical cause. Being a Christian, he recommended her to talk over her difficulties with a counsellor.

During counselling, the girl came to see that she was afraid to let go of her fears, for she lived by the attention that her physical problems brought her. She was so insecure that she could not live without attention. She 'enjoyed' bad health. The counsellor helped her face the fact that in Christ she was eternally secure, and this insight, though but feebly and dimly apprehended at first, grew in her heart, until her attention-getting sicknesses dropped away.

There's a price to being well. Are you sure you can pay it? Being well means facing up to life's responsibilities, going back to work, dealing with those pressing problems, facing harsh realities, and living without any special attention.

It helps greatly, too, in the quest for healing if one has a purpose to be well. Sten Nilsson, a Swedish missionary, tells how, as a young boy, he was very ill, and he overheard the doctor say to his mother, 'You need not send for me to make out the death certificate. I'll write it out now.' When Sten heard that, he said to himself, 'I do not intend to die: I intend to be a missionary to India.' The next day he got up from his bed, and was soon a picture of health!

What I am talking about here must be seen as a major step in the quest for healing. There must be a willingness to face up to the subterfuges that go on inside us, and a desire to have done with make-believe, camouflage and escapism. Complete openness and honesty is vital. Nothing can atone for lack of it.

I am not suggesting, of course, that this is the case with everyone, but it is certainly worth exploring whenever we fall prey to sickness. So ask yourself: do I really want to get well? Am I willing to go back into life and accept its responsibilities? Am I prepared, with God's help, to adjust to all that life has to offer me? Can I accept robust health at Christ's hands so that no one will ever need to feel sorry for me again?

This clear-cut decision of the will to ask and answer such questions fearlessly and honestly is vitally important, for without this you may never find yourself on the road to health again.

6. *Ask God in prayer to heal you*

Whether you are receiving medical attention or believing that God will heal you supernaturally, it is always appropriate to put yourself in an attitude of expectancy by prayerfully asking God to bring about your complete healing.

After all, as I have pointed out earlier, although doctors can prescribe remedies, and although they can cut away diseased tissues and graft in new ones, only God can heal.

How then should we pray for healing to take place? With positive faith and in complete confidence that it is the Father's will to heal us.

If you have followed carefully the concepts I have presented in this book so far, then you will have realized that before one can positively pray for healing, certain factors have to be brought into focus.

For example:

> You must be convinced that God wills your health.
>
> You must throw overboard attitudes that hinder the flow of God's healing power. These attitudes cover a wide range, but the four most disruptive ones, as we saw, were fear, resentment, guilt and self-centredness.
>
> You must be alert as to what prevents people from being healed so that you can overcome these barriers.
>
> You must face yourself with scrupulous honesty and

decide whether or not you really want to get well. This means adopting the same attitude as the Psalmist when he prayed: 'Search me, O God, and know my heart: try me, and know my thoughts' (Ps 139:23, AV).

You must adopt an active and not a passive stance towards your illness. Stand up to it in the knowledge that God is on your side. The Almighty wills your health, now *you* will it too.

Now, having settled these issues, pray a prayer similar to this:

Heavenly Father, I come to you through the name of Jesus Christ, your only begotten Son, who bore all my sins and all my sicknesses on the cross of Calvary. Your word says that by his stripes we are healed. So now, dear Father, on the basis of your word, I come to you to ask you to heal me of my sickness. I confess every sin, every wrong attitude and action, every fear, every resentment, everything that is not of you, and I claim the promise of your word that also says: 'Whatsoever you shall ask in my name, I will do it.' I ask now that this sickness, this infirmity, this disease shall be removed from my body in your name and by your power. Destroy its hold on my life and set me free from it in the name of Jesus. I am thankful that when I pray in the name of Jesus, you have promised to always hear me, and so, dear Lord, heal me now, for the praise and honour and glory of your peerless and precious name. Thank you, Father. Amen.

Once you have prayed and asked God to heal you, then rest in the confidence that God has heard you and that his healing work has begun. 'This is the assurance we have in approaching God, that if we ask anything according to his will, he hears us. And if we know that he hears us—whatever we ask—we know that we have what we asked of him' (1 Jn 5:14–15, NIV).

Keep in mind, too, that not all healings are sudden. Sometimes God heals instantly and other times, gradually. Both are to be received with praise. Do not be discouraged or disappointed if there is no immediate improvement. Unrealized by you, it may have already begun.

8   'There's a Lot More to Health Than Not Being Sick'

The subject of healing, as we have seen, is of vital importance to every Christian, but what is equally important is the subject of *health*. In this chapter, therefore, I propose to look beyond the issue of healing to the wider issue of what constitutes true health.

Over the past few years a strange new term has appeared on the medical horizon. The term is 'holistic health'. The word 'holistic' is a synonym for 'wholeness', and the term 'holistic health' is used to describe the health of the whole person—physically, mentally and emotionally.

Some Christian doctors, because of the tendency of secularists to introduce questionable approaches such as hypnotism, acupuncture, etc. into holistic medicine, are veering away from the word, and instead are using the phrase 'whole-person medicine'—a sentiment with which I entirely agree.

The phrase was coined several years ago when a number of doctors and medical specialists began to see that instead of just treating illness or disease, they should be treating people. At an international conference on health, one doctor said: 'In the past, we doctors treated diseases that happened to be in people: in the future, we need to learn how to treat people who happen to have diseases.'

The growing conviction in the medical world that the interrelatedness between mind and body ought to be taken more seriously has been described by someone as a new era in medicine. More and more doctors are recognizing that the quality of our relationships and our inner attitudes may have more to do with why we became ill than our genes, our diet, or our environment.

Treating disease is not enough

If you visited your doctor to discuss a physical problem, he would probably tell you (if you asked him) that most of your body was well. However disturbing the affected part, or however much discomfort it may cause, it is probably true to say that it is due to a breakdown in one small part of your physical frame.

The doctor, unless he is whole-person minded, would not concern himself with your inner attitudes or attempt to get you involved in a body-building course, but would focus on treating the part of your body that is affected. He would attempt to bring about healing in that one specific area.

Therein lies a problem. Most doctors in the Western world, generally speaking, have been trained to focus on treating diseases rather than on promoting health. One doctor, after leaving medical school, said that he and his colleagues seemed to be practising 'end organ medicine'. When asked to explain, he said: 'A problem that begins with a destructive lifestyle, or with negative relationships, finally affects the body, moving from one system to another, until it stops at some particular organ with nowhere else to go. We then pronounce the organ defective, either treating it, or moving it.'

Some Eastern cultures, both past and present, maintain that when a person becomes ill, treatment must be directed towards the whole person, and although some of the methods they employ in doing this would not meet with Western approval, they certainly are on the right track when it comes to seeing a person as a whole.

One ancient Chinese culture records that the doctor in a community was paid only when everyone was well, and penalized when people became sick. This was because the community saw the doctor's task as working with them to maintain a healthy balance between body and mind.

A growing number of medical experts are beginning to see the unproductiveness of an approach that focuses only on the area of malfunction, and are open to an alternative approach. The answer, so I believe, lies in 'whole-person medicine'—treatment that concerns itself not only with the physical aspects of a person, but with his mental, spiritual and emotional aspects also.

Health is more than the absence of sickness

The study of illness and disease is of the utmost importance, but if we knew everything there is to know about disease and how it should be treated, it would not necessarily produce health. As the whole-person health practitioners are continually saying, 'There's a lot more to health than not being sick.'

People can be pronounced fit at their annual check-up and then drop dead within a few weeks. Health is much more than the absence of sickness: it is the *presence* of something. What that 'something' is, is difficult to define. Let's call it, for the moment, a positive flow of life and energy that co-ordinates the physical, mental and emotional aspects of man, and enables them to function together as a harmonious whole.

Where does this life-giving energy come from? Most non-Christians would not believe it, but it comes directly from Jesus Christ who is the creator and sustainer of the universe. Scripture puts it like this:

> For by him all things were created: things in heaven and on earth, visible and invisible, whether thrones or powers or rulers or authorities; all things were created by him and for him. He is before all things, and in him all things hold together (Col 1:16–18, NIV).

In the Old Testament the godless King Belshazzar thought that he was independent of God, and believed that he owed his existence to no one but himself. God confronted him on one occasion with these words: 'And you...Belshazzar...have not been humble. For you have defied the Lord of Heaven...you have not praised the God who gives you the breath of life and controls your destiny!' (Dan 5:22–24, TLB.)

God's life supports and sustains every person on the face of the earth. As the God of providence, he not only created men and women, but he sustains them also. But the life of which I am now speaking is *natural* life, the life that equips a man to relate to the earthly environment.

There is another aspect of life that also comes from God, through his Son Jesus Christ—*spiritual* life. This is given only in response to faith. When a person receives Jesus Christ as his Lord and Saviour and Jesus Christ is allowed to reside in the human heart, then (potentially at least) all parts of the personality are drawn to health.

A non-Christian may experience life, but he cannot experience the *abundant* life of which Christ speaks in John 10:10. Prior to conversion, a human being has all the potential for functioning as God designed him, but the parts of his personality lack a co-ordinating factor. When Christ comes in, he seeks, given our consent and co-operation, to bring all parts of the personality to health.

This is why I believe that true health and wholeness can only be found in God.

Traditional medicine versus whole-person medicine

The concept of wholeness, or, as some people call it, 'wellness', may, in due course, bring about a revolution in the training of medical practitioners. Up until now medical students have been trained to concentrate on pathology (the study of disease) rather than on the positive aspects of health. Perhaps some comparisons between traditional medicine and whole-person medicine might help to clarify this issue:

In traditional medicine the model followed is that of a doctor and a patient. The doctor is active, the patient is passive. In whole-person medicine the patient is encouraged to be active, by engaging in behaviour and attitudes that work towards wholeness.

In traditional medicine the goal is that of getting rid of illness and disease. In whole-person medicine the goal is that of achieving a high degree of 'wellness'.

In traditional medicine the focus of concentration is on the affected part. In whole-person medicine the focus of concentration is on the whole person and his lifestyle.

In traditional medicine diagnosis is limited to physical factors only. In whole-person medicine diagnosis is concerned with all parts of the personality.

In traditional medicine specialist help is obtained from those whose training falls into the category of dealing with physiological disorders. In whole-person medicine specialist help is obtained from those trained in other disciplines, such as psychology, religion and so on.

At a conference I attended in Denver, Colorado, a few years ago, two doctors, speaking on 'holistic-health', defined it in this way: 'Holistic medicine is helping a person maximize the wellness potential of which he is capable.'

They went on to say that in their own practice they were committed to nurturing people towards wellness rather than simply dealing with illnesses that required treatment.

Howard Clinebell, professor of pastoral psychology and counselling at Claremont Graduate School, California, speaking of the holistic approach to health says: 'Health professionals should go into the community and teach people how to achieve high level wellness rather than waiting until they get sick. The technology of modern medicine, oriented to treating gross pathology and trauma by surgery, powerful drugs and space-age technology, has little to do with either the degree of wellness of individuals or the general level of wellness in society.'

Jesus—a whole-person healer

Jesus, the most wonderful healer the world has ever seen, did not just focus on sickness and disease, and make that the full scope of his ministry, as, I am sorry to say, many present-day healing evangelists do.

Christ's ministry of healing was incidental to his preaching and teaching ministry. Although he had great

110

'THERE'S A LOT MORE TO HEALTH THAN...'

compassion for the sick, as evidenced by his many miracles, he longed not simply to make people better, but to make them whole.

In his preaching and teaching, therefore, he took great care to lay down the principles through which men and women could achieve wholeness. His Sermon on the Mount, for example, contains statements and principles, which, if followed, lay down in the personality a solid foundation for physical, mental and spiritual health.

Some time ago I came across one of the most challenging statements I think I have ever read. It came from the pen of a noted psychiatrist, Dr James C. Fisher. After fifty years of practice, dealing with all kinds of mental and emotional problems, he wrote:

> I dreamed of writing a handbook that would be simple, practical, easy to understand, easy to follow. It would tell people how to live—what thoughts and attitudes and philosophies to cultivate, and what pitfalls to avoid in seeking mental health. I attended every symposium it was possible for me to attend and took notes on the wise words of my colleagues who were leaders in their field. And quite by accident I discovered that such a work had been completed!
>
> If you were to take the sum total of all authoritative articles ever written by the most qualified of psychologists and psychiatrists on the subject of mental hygiene—if you were to combine them and refine them and cleave out the excess verbiage—if you were to take the whole of the meat and none of the parsley, and if you were to have these unadulterated bits of pure scientific knowledge concisely expressed by the most capable of living poets you would have an awkward and incomplete summation of the summation of the Sermon on the Mount. And it would suffer immeasurably through the comparison. For nearly two thousand years the Christian world has been holding in its hands the complete answer to its restless and fruitless yearnings. Here...rests the blueprint for successful human

111

life with optimum mental health and contentment.

Christ's central emphasis was on the salvation of the soul not the healing of the body. If we ignore this fact, then we can become bogged down with just getting rid of sickness. But after we have done that what have we got to put in its place?

We must be careful we do not make Christianity a healing cult, for its primary purpose is not to deliver us from sickness, but to make us whole. And this is best achieved by the development of a right relationship to God, a right relationship to oneself and a right relationship to others. Jesus made it clear by his words and ministry that once we find salvation for our soul, then physical well-being becomes a by-product.

Doctors in a dilemma

One question being asked by many doctors here in the West is this: what can we do for those whose physical problems are so obviously rooted in the emotions?

While doing some research work for this book, an astonishing piece of writing fell into my hands. It was a report on a recent survey by the American Medical Association in which several thousand general practitioners across the country were asked this question: 'What percentage of people you see in a week have needs that you are qualified to treat with your skills?'

Some replied 25%, some 1%, but the average was 10%. On this estimate 90% of the people who see a general practitioner in an average week have no medically treatable problem. Does this mean they are malingering and just pretending to be unwell? No. They are ill all right, but their sickness has no traceable physiological cause.

The survey went on to ask what were some of the ways doctors attempted to help such people whose problems were not physically or chemically based. Most of the doctors said they prescribed tranquillizers. When asked what steps they would take to help people if *they had the time*, most of the doctors said they would like to spend an hour talking to such patients about their work, their lifestyle, their problems and their families.

A doctor I know here in Britain has already begun to put into practice the principles underlying holistic health. Whenever he comes across a patient who is obviously in need of more than physical attention, he says something like this, 'Look, I would love to be able to spend some time talking to you about your problems and difficulties because, in my view, these are contributing to your physical problem. My time, however, is greatly limited, as you can see from my waiting room, but I have a few friends not far from here who would be willing to sit down with you and help you with your problems. If you would like to take advantage of this service, it's completely free, and is run by a few members of the church I attend. Let me know and I will set up an appointment for you.'

His friends are trained and experienced Christian counsellors who work, not from the church premises, but from an ordinary house. Without pushing Christianity down people's throats, they listen and share the advice they feel they can give—advice that is based on biblical principles.

He told me that, time and time again, patients referred to the counselling centre in this way come back to him radically changed. They may not be converted, for that is not the aim of the service, but they certainly are impressed with the love and care that was shown them. My own views of such a service is that it becomes, in

God's hands, a marvellous introduction to the spirit that underlies Christianity—the spirit that nurtures, cherishes and *cares*.

A few years ago a group of Christian doctors and medical specialists got together, here in Britain, to form what is now known as the Caring Professions Concern. Their goal is to help the members of their profession move towards a more whole-person approach. The work they are doing is, in my view, one of the most exciting projects I have ever come across.

They envisage a number of health centres across the country, integrated with local churches, where Christians and non-Christians can experience whole-person caring —caring that concerns itself not just with eliminating the negative (illness and disease), but adding the positive (right attitudes, right insights and right lifestyle).

May their tribe increase!

Caring in the Christian community

The more I become acquainted with the principles of whole-person health, the more I realize that the church holds one of the keys to health which, regrettably, it is not using. The timing is right for Christians who take spiritual things seriously to develop a biblical approach to caring in the local church, and to move towards an in-depth counselling ministry for those whose lives are tangled up by problems and difficulties.

Dr Lawrence Crabb, a psychologist who gave up a lucrative practice in order to teach Christians to counsel, believes that too. He says:

> I am convinced that the local church should and can success-
> fully assume responsibility within its ranks for restoring
> troubled people to full productive, creative lives. One

psychiatrist recently commented that his patients are all basically hungry for love and acceptance. Where should true love be more evident than in a local church? Jesus prayed that his people would be one. Paul speaks of rejoicing and weeping with one another and bearing each other's burdens. To the degree that our Lord's design for his church is implemented, the deep need for love which, if unmet, generates psychological problems, will be satisfied within the church.

Crabb believes that the local church is uniquely designed to minister to the needs of emotionally upset people. He claims that if the church is functioning correctly, using its God-given ministries, it is possible to bring help and healing even to those that society labels psychotic.

It is my belief that one of the greatest needs in the contemporary Christian scene is the establishing of an efficient counselling ministry in every congregation of Christ's people. Let me give you a picture of what can happen when a local church seeks to meet its responsibility of providing a caring ministry for those who are distressed and in need.

This church sent several of its ministry team to an Institute in Christian Counselling conducted by Crusade for World Revival. After training, they opened up a counselling centre in their church, and let it be known that they were prepared to try and help anyone who wanted to talk to them about their problems.

One day, one of the church members walked in and said, 'I'm at my wits' end. My doctor says there is nothing wrong with me yet I have all kinds of physical difficulties. My head aches, it feels as if there is a steel band around it, my joints ache, and it's got so bad that I can't do my work.' The conversation then went something like this:

Counsellor: Help me get a picture of what is going on

115

	in your life, particularly in the area of your thoughts. If I could tape-record your brain, what are the kind of thoughts I would pick up?
Counsellee:	Well, it's difficult to say. Most of my thoughts are negative ones.
Counsellor:	Such as?
Counsellee:	Things like: 'What's the use of trying. Nobody seems to understand me.'
Counsellor:	Anything else?
Counsellee:	Yes. I get thoughts about suicide... thoughts about sex...thoughts about Christianity being nothing more than a myth...and so on.
Counsellor:	Looks like you're having a real battle with your thought life. I have plenty of time so what I would like you to do is to just sit there and share with me all your fears, your worries and your concerns. I'm a good listener and I care.

When after about an hour and a half the counsellee had aired his fears and his worries, and before the counsellor could make any comment, he sat back in his chair and said: 'Wait a minute. Don't say anything. I see it all now so clearly. I've been concentrating on the negative things that have been going on in my life. I have overlooked the positive things God has been doing for me. He has given me a fine family, a lovely wife, a caring church, a good job, and here I am concentrating on the difficulties but forgetting the blessings. You don't need to say any more. I'm going out of here to face the problems in my life and beat them—with God's help. Thank you so much for doing what you did to help me.'

In some ways the counsellor did very little, but he had

been doing the one thing that counsellors should excel at: *listening*. Within a week, the counsellor learned that the man's distressing symptoms had disappeared and he was functioning normally again.

It's amazing how our health improves when we have an opportunity to share with someone who cares just what is going on inside us. Can you see the tremendous potential that lies within the church of Jesus Christ for helping people towards wholeness?

The church of Jesus Christ, when functioning in harmony with God's principles, can do as much, if not more, to bring about wholeness as the skills of doctors. The majority of people who are experiencing physical problems can be tremendously helped by the warm, genuine interest of people who care.

So let the church take its place in this movement towards health and wholeness. God is on the side of health. So should we be too.

New kinds of hospitals

In some parts of the world there are hospitals whose facilities include ways in which they can minister to the emotional as well as the physical needs of their patients. I do not mean psychiatric units, but therapy rooms where people with ordinary, everyday problems can talk over their difficulties with someone who understands and cares.

Irene Kraus, an official of the American Hospital Association, in her book *The Importance of Caring*, says: 'Compassionate, personalized care has long remained the ultimate goal of hospitals. In fact, in the early days of hospitals and medicines, caring was often a sole aid that physicians and nurses could give to their patients. Many diseases had no cure, medical capabilities to relieve suffering were limited. Because cures were not possible, caring was the only alternative.'

A retired nursing sister, when I quoted those words of Irene Kraus to her, said wistfully, 'I well remember the days when, because we had so few cures, we had to compensate by huge doses of tender loving care. Today with so many instant cures, such as modern drugs can achieve, hospitals have become like factories.' That is very sad, but true.

However, there is hope. If the movement towards whole-person medicine gets off the ground, and there are signs that at the moment it seems to be doing well, then within the foreseeable future we may find ourselves being treated by doctors and nurses to whom emotional caring is as important as physical caring.

Irene Kraus goes on to say: 'The principles of compassion and helpful care are based in part on the spiritual values of religion and in part on the moral values important in the philosophy of a democratic nation. Both principles proclaim the inherent value and dignity of each man. So all hospitals, not just religion-based institutions, are responsible to the community for humanistic care.'

The biting challenge of her argument is not just that all hospitals should assume responsibility for humanistic care, but that only people with deep spiritual values are inwardly motivated to provide that care. Of course, there will be humanists who will argue that a person does not need to have religious values to be able to care, and to some extent they are right, but history shows us that wherever there has been a concern for life and health and well-being, the church has been in the forefront.

What is the main thing that emerges from this new era in medicine, the movement towards wholeness? It is this: medical doctors are needed when the symptoms of illness and disease are detected, but the responsibility for maintaining health belongs to us. To a certain extent, we must become our own doctors.

This may be a good counterbalance to the past tendency to elevate a doctor to an almost omnipotent position in matters of health, where we expect him to wave a magic wand and make us well again. Whether we recover from sickness and move towards health depends not only on a physician's skill, but on our own inner attitudes, our lifestyle and acceptance of some personal responsibility.

The development of such attitudes will be the subject of the next chapter.

9 *A Prescription for Health*

Just before his hundred and twentieth birthday, Moses, the great leader of the children of Israel, said to his people: 'I call heaven and earth to witness against you this day, that I have set before you life and death, blessing and curse; therefore *choose life*, that you and your descendants may live' (Deut 30:19, RSV, author's italics).

'Choose life.' Are we really able to do that? Aren't we victims of our environment, subject to such things as germs, genes and hereditary forces? Well, to some extent, of course, we are, but with God's help we can choose to be whole people. We can't always avoid sickness or illness, but we can begin to practise the principles that lead to health and wholeness. We can 'choose life'.

In this chapter, I want to talk to you not about sickness, but about health. We are going to explore some of the attitudes and behaviours that, when practised, make a positive contribution to good health and well-being.

If, as we have been seeing, our mental beliefs and frame of mind are so influential in this matter of health, then it follows that we ought to choose the attitudes that build up rather than break down our health. After all, as one doctor put it, 'You're as healthy as your attitudes, not just your arteries.'

What, then, are the most vital attitudes we can develop that make a positive contribution to health? There are many. I have selected what, in my judgement, are the seven most important. I wouldn't be surprised if some of them are already well established in your mind.

Think health

If our thoughts penetrate to the marrow of our bones, then let those thoughts be thoughts of health, not of disease. You can think health or think disease into the very inmost cells of your being. So think health.

I do not believe that you can get rid of sickness by mere affirmation, but the mind does have a tremendous influence upon the body and its health.

Some may consider this to be auto-suggestion. Well, in a way, it is. But we are always suggesting things to ourselves, so why not let the thing we suggest be health? That is auto-suggestion without self-deception.

And why? Because the body in its inner structure is made for health, not disease. When our physical frame was designed by God in the beginning, his purpose was for it to be healthy, and he provided it with every contrivance possible to ward off disease. So when we think health, we are really thinking God's thoughts after him.

When we think disease, however, we are thinking contrary to God's purpose. When we think health, we are aligning ourselves with the healing forces of the universe—indeed, with the Creator himself.

A family who lived in the little mining village where I was brought up spent most of their time together recounting their various ailments. Whenever I was with them, I would feel depressed because they would say such things as this: I've spent the whole day struggling to overcome this pain in my back.' Another would say: 'My problem has been an ache in my side.'

This was usually the cue for the other members of the family to discuss their various aches and pains. There were some occasions when I even felt like inventing a few personal difficulties myself—just to be part of the scene!

This family lived, talked and thought sickness and disease. The consequence of this was that they all died before their time with the exception of one who married a nurse! Fortunately, she taught him that it's just as easy to think health as it is disease.

I know it is not always possible to think in terms of health, especially if you are confronted by disease in yourself or in others. But it depends where your gaze is fixed. One famous doctor had a motto on his desk that read: 'Glance at disease—gaze at health.' As he specialized in treating patients who had trouble with their hearts, real and imaginary, he kept a model of a healthy heart before him in his office.

He said that this constantly reminded him of a healthy heart instead of a diseased one. It kept his vision clear. I am told that when some medical students first begin to study the heart and its diseases, they sometimes develop the symptoms they study. Then they right themselves and fix their eyes on health-giving influences. They begin to think health instead of disease.

Over a doughnut shop was this sign:

> As you ramble through life my brother,
>   Whatever may be your goal,
> Keep your eye upon the doughnut,
>   And not upon the hole.

So get your eyes off the 'hole' of sickness and disease—

and focus it on the 'doughnut' of health and wholeness. Think health!

Be happy

If you are a Christian then it's your birthright to be happy, apart from specific occasions that cause sadness for a while. God not only wills your health, but he wills your happiness too. He couldn't be God and will anything else.

You may be saying, especially if you are of phlegmatic temperament like me, 'Being happy is easier said than done.' But it's amazing how you can cultivate happiness when you focus your mind in the right direction.

Our emotions follow our thoughts just like baby ducks follow their mother. When we have the right attitudes, then our emotions respond by producing the right feelings. Life may be serious, but don't treat it more seriously than it ought to be. Learn to laugh at things that don't really matter that much.

A missionary tells of how she went back to her lonely station in the interior of Japan after the Second World War. Food was very scarce, but one day someone gave her two slices of bacon, which at that time was regarded as a luxury.

She invited a friend, a little Japanese girl, to have breakfast with her. However, while frying the bacon, she was distracted for a few moments by a neighbour's call. When she returned, the two pieces of bacon were burned black. She fought back the tears, and then smiled and said to her friend: 'Let's have a good laugh.'

And they did, laughing while they ate the charred bits. They made a game of it!

When things don't seem to work out right, why not have a good laugh. It's surprising how easily this attitude can be cultivated when you decide to look at life through different eyes.

I had a long argument some years ago with a man who insisted that happiness is not a matter of conscious choice. I took the view that it was, and he spent many hours trying to convince me differently. I am still of the opinion, to this day, that happiness is something that can be cultivated.

We can, to a large extent, make up our minds to be happy—or miserable. There are times in my own life when things begin to get me down, and then I remember the advice I am now giving you—and throw back my head and laugh.

One medical specialist is reported as saying: 'You can't kill a happy man.' When pressed for an explanation, he said that unhappiness often precedes sickness. Happy people rarely become ill, and tend to recover quickly when they do. The unhappy person is a target for many kinds of illnesses.

Norman Cousins, in his book *Anatomy of an Illness as Perceived by the Patient*, tells how one day he was informed by his doctors that his fast-developing paralysis was untreatable. He was told that his chances for recovery were 1 in 500. Cousins asked his doctor's permission to treat his own illness, and this was granted.

First, he moved out of the hospital into an hotel. He then began to read up on stress-related illnesses, and began to dose himself with vitamin C. Somewhere he had read that laughter was therapeutic, so he decided to engage in as much laughter as he could each day. He hired old films like *Candid Camera* and the Marx Brothers, and for several hours a day he sat and laughed.

The monitoring machines he set up to keep a check on him showed that laughing had improved his health. 'Ten minutes of belly laughter,' he said, 'gave me an hour of pain-free sleep. The more I laughed, the better I got.' In time his symptoms disappeared, and he went back to work.

Now he tells the world, not only through his best-selling book, but also by teaching in medical schools, how laughter helped him to recovery. Doctors say that Cousins' self-prescribed therapy of happiness has a scientific basis. Laughter triggers endozymes that are natural morphine-like pain-killers. With laughter as his pain-killer, Norman Cousins no longer had to use drugs that interfere with the body's own internal healing system. Laughter, he claims, helped him get well.

The Bible tells us that 'A cheerful heart is a good medicine, but a downcast spirit dries up the bones' (Prov 17:22, RSV). Grimness is not a Christian virtue. 'Joy,' as Pierre Teilhard de Chardin puts it, 'is the surest sign of the presence of God.'

Let your mind dwell constantly on the fact that God is your Father; Jesus, your Saviour; the Holy Spirit, your Comforter; the Bible, your guide; heaven, your reward; and eternity, your goal. And, if that is not enough to make you happy, then remind yourself that God is working in your life to turn all negatives into positives, all setbacks into springboards and all stumbling blocks into stepping stones.

This is his promise in Romans 8:28. Think about it—and be happy!

Live creatively

Most of us, if we are honest, prefer to settle for a nice, quiet, safe and comfortable life. Almost from the moment we come into the world, we are told to 'play it safe', 'don't take risks'. It's no wonder that so many of us tread a safe and predictable path.

God is a creator, and when he made us he stamped us with his own divine image—we are to be creators, too. Mini-creators, but *creators* nevertheless.

How creative are you? Do you search out new ways of doing things, explore new frontiers, and develop your potential to its utmost limits? Someone has described Jesus as the great awakener—and he is. Paul speaks of 'all the stimulus of Christ' (Phil 2:1, MOFFATT).

Contact with Jesus Christ stimulates the creative centre in each one of us if we let him, making us aware of God and the infinite possibilities in God.

I was extremely backward in school until I met Jesus Christ, always bottom of the class. I said to myself, a few weeks after I was converted, 'This is no place for a Christian,' and left it.

Someone, describing their experience of living in a new city, said, 'It's so exciting. I think I have covered everything when, bang—there goes another horizon!' If we really get close to Jesus Christ, and see life from his point of view, then we will come out with the same conclusion—bang, there goes another horizon!

In our Lord's company, we should begin to see farther, feel for people on a wider scale and act more decisively. We will say with Jesus, 'Weep not for me—I'm not asking for your compassion or sympathy. I am moving towards an open door, a new task—the greatest challenge of my life.'

And remember, it is never too late to be a creative personality. The idea that we retire at sixty-five is a cultural invention that has been responsible for putting people in their graves long before their time. My advice to you is never retire. Circumstances may force you to leave your job or profession at sixty or sixty-five, but that doesn't mean you must stop being creative.

A famous writer claims that old age is something

invented by men. 'God,' he says, 'never invented old age. Death is his gift to those who have lived a full life. His intention is for us to die young at an advanced age.'

A professor's wife, who didn't know one end of an artist's paintbrush from the other, said to herself at the age of sixty: 'I wonder what gifts are lying undeveloped and unexplored within me.' She prayed that God might guide her, and within a few days someone gave her a box of artist's painting materials. As she started to use them, something awakened within her, and today her paintings of Bible scenes are the fond possessions of many Christian families.

Don't, I beg of you, live a life of dull routine. Within you lie all kinds of potential which, with the proper approach and the right attitude, can be released and made to work towards creative ends. To be creative may mean that you will have to shake yourself free of those cautious attitudes you have built up over the years. It may scare you half to death to think of moving beyond the *status quo*. But do it anyway.

Remember, the creative impulse comes from a creative God.

Love everybody

Some years ago Smiley Blanton, a psychologist, wrote a book entitled *Love or Perish*. In it he made the claim that unless we love others enough to share ourselves with them, then something dies on the inside of us. To live effectively in this world, he said, we must love.

He was mainly thinking in psychological terms, but when we look into the Scriptures we find a similar theme there. Love, said the apostle Paul in that famous thirteenth chapter of 1 Corinthians, is the quality that endures and survives the ages.

What then is love? How can we define the term? There have been endless definitions of the word, but let me share with you Bruce Larson's definition: 'Love is making the people you relate to feel important when they are around you.'

He says: 'You can't convince me you are a loving person if the person you are trying to love does not feel important when around you.' That's what love is all about, he claims, making others feel that they are on the receiving end of something fine and noble and beautiful.

Jesus loved like that. When he was with people, he respected them for who they were, irrespective of whether or not he agreed with their lifestyle. Christ had the ability to differentiate between sin and the sinner. He was *for* the sinner, but *against* the sin.

Read the Gospels, and watch how Christ asks questions of people—and then watch him as he listens to their answers. He wants to know what they are thinking about themselves, about their problems or about him. And, believe me, there is no better way of making people feel they are valued than by listening to them. If we love people, we will listen to them.

But many of us are so intent on telling people about ourselves that we have no time to listen. If we want to love in the same way that Jesus loved, then we must take a leaf out of his book—and learn to listen.

Some Christians have told me, 'It's difficult for me to love because when I was a child I was exposed to an unloving atmosphere. Because I did not receive love, I am unable to give it.' I usually refer them to 1 John 4:19 which says: 'We love... because he first loved us.' No Christian can say that he is not the subject of love, when the greatest Lover in the universe, the Lord Jesus Christ, has lavished his love upon him.

Our task, as Christ's followers, is to love as we have

been loved. And that means making people feel valued and important when they are around us.

'Many sicknesses and illnesses come upon us,' said a psychiatrist, 'not because of the bad things that happen to us but because so few good things happen to us.'

Today or tomorrow you may meet someone to whom very few good things have happened. The love of Jesus flowing through you to them can be like the little branches people cling to as they climb life's mountain trail.

And your love might be the window through which they catch a glimpse of that greater love—the love of Jesus.

Live one day at a time

Jesus showed very penetrating insight when he said: 'So never be troubled about tomorrow; tomorrow will take care of itself. The day's own trouble is enough for the day' (Mt 6:34, MOFFATT).

He was not saying that there are no troubles to be faced—there are. Life is bound to bring trouble. But don't telescope the troubles of tomorrow into today. Meet today, today, says Jesus, for if you bring the troubles of tomorrow into today your anticipation of them will overwhelm your ability to handle one day's problems at a time. You are making two sets of troubles out of one—the trouble before it comes and when it actually happens.

However, Jesus is not saying here that we ought not to plan for the days that lie ahead and anticipate things, but that we should refrain from bringing the *concern* of tomorrow's problems into today.

Such a telescoping of trouble causes a double expenditure of energy, and it is quite pointless. 'Worry,' said someone, 'is the advance interest we pay on troubles that might never come.' Some of them, of course, do come, but when they do, you can meet them and conquer them a day at a time. Tomorrow's troubles, plus today's, can overwhelm you.

Before commencing work on this chapter, I asked a doctor friend of mine what he considered to be the biggest single cause of the psychosomatic problems of his patients.

He thought for a few minutes, and said, 'Worry.' I pressed him for a fuller answer. 'Well,' he said, 'people don't realize that they have enough energy to meet any problem, provided they view it a day at a time. All the energies can be gathered up in constructive achievement, but when tomorrow's concerns are brought into today, then the distraction produces destruction.'

How much of our sickness, I wonder, is either brought on or compounded by bringing tomorrow into today.

Let's step back and look at this issue as objectively as we can. Today is the tomorrow you worried about yesterday. Today isn't so bad, is it? It has troubles, but they are bearable. Even at its worst, today is bearable.

If the whole day seems difficult, then do what a friend of mine does—divide it up into hours. Then meet each hour with your full resources—your faith in God, your reliance upon him and the energy he provides.

Say over and over again to yourself: 'In quietness and confidence shall be my strength.' Note the two things there—quietness and confidence. You must quiet everything in the presence of God. Still your whole being before him and drink in his quiet strength. Allow his healing power to penetrate every pore of your being, bathing the tired, restless nerve cells with his energy-building power.

Quietness is passive, but notice now the other side—confidence. Confidence is active. Break down the word and what do you find? *Con*—'with', *fideo*—'faith'. It is not faith on its own, but your faith plus God's faith. Your faith and God's faith flow together, and when that happens, then every situation can be faced. And not only faced, but turned to good ends.

So why needlessly burden yourself by bringing tomorrow's problems into today? Follow the advice of Jesus and meet today, today.

Admit when you are wrong

It may be hard for some to see the connection between good health and the willingness to admit when you are wrong, but such a connection is there, nevertheless.

Often what is found in those suffering from emotional or mental illness is the tendency towards self-justification. I know that anecdotes prove nothing, but in my experience as a minister, now stretching well over thirty years, I have noticed how those with deep mental or emotional problems struggle to justify themselves in the eyes of others.

Once when visiting a patient in a psychiatric hospital outside Wakefield, I asked one of the doctors what were the chances of this particular patient getting well. He said what at the time I considered to be an astonishing thing, but I have lived to see the sense of his remarks: 'John will not start wanting to get well until he stops wanting to be right.'

What are you like in relation to this matter of wanting to be right? Is it hard for you to say, 'I was wrong,' when you know it to be so. Maintaining the feeling of being right will take its toll on you, physically, emotionally and spiritually.

'The inordinate need to be right,' says a Christian counsellor, 'is a block to the whole and healthy life God wants to give us. It takes a lot of psychic energy to maintain this constant posture of rightness, and eventually our bodies are going to pay the price for the stress that results.'

One of the most pathetic figures of this century is Richard Nixon—ex-president of the United States. It is the opinion of many that, had he not been so vehement in his defence, the problems of 'Watergate' would not have brought about his removal from office. His self-justification, in the face of what so many considered was undeniable guilt, so deeply offended the American public that they demanded his resignation.

Almost all of his friends deserted him, and one American, commenting on his predicament some time later, said, 'I believe Richard Nixon is a poignant illustration of the disastrous results of being unable to say, "I was wrong."'

Just as physical healing can only take place in an atmosphere of openness (a person must admit they have a wound before it can be treated), so inner health can only develop when a person is willing to admit to self-justification if it is there, and permit the great Physician to remove it.

Dr Salvador Minuchin, the founder of Family Therapy, a system of counselling that involves all members of the family unit, claims that any member of a family who has emotional problems has not got into that situation alone. He has experienced a breakdown within the family group, and all members of the family have a responsibility to bear (so he claims) when one member suffers.

His approach, when counselling, is to bring all the members of the family together and examine their relationships one with the other. He usually finds that the emotional problem in a particular member of the family is caused or compounded by the way they are relating to each other as a whole. And one of the commonest contributing factors in physical or emotional illness, according to Dr Minuchin, is the family who will not allow someone else to be wrong.

'The patient,' he says, 'is often the product of an overprotective family who keep excusing or apologizing for him or her.' It's very difficult, he says, to help a patient free themselves from the family who insists on supporting or defending them.

This used to be my big problem in the early part of my life and ministry. I think in some ways it was a crucial factor in bringing about the strange illness that nearly took my life. My wife used to say to me, whenever we had an argument, 'Your trouble is that you will never admit it when you are wrong.'

She was absolutely right. When I learned to say, 'I'm sorry, I was wrong,' it had a positive effect on my whole being, physically as well as spiritually. Now I'm not defensive about my failures or my mistakes. I own up to them willingly.

And, believe me, I feel a lot better for it.

Get rid of resentments

Walter Alvarez, a doctor and a specialist, says, 'Resentments and anger put the whole physical and mental system on a war basis, instead of a peace basis. If you live on a war basis all the time then you are a drained personality.'

I once saw a man, an official in a church I once pastored, gradually kill himself, simply by refusing to give up his resentments. He had nothing but hatred towards a man who had wronged him, and although I talked to him about it, and begged him to take the way of Christ and forgive, he refused. Within two years of harbouring his bitterness, he was dead. His doctor told me that he had 'choked on his resentments'.

Is it true that resentments can cause physical sickness or illness? A woman once told me that she disliked her husband so intensely that whenever he came home at night, she would break out in rose-like blotches. 'He burns me up,' she said. But all she succeeded in doing by her resentments was burn herself up.

I read a few days ago of the case of a man who was quite healthy but who became involved in a lawsuit. He could think and talk of nothing else. His family pleaded with him to cool his resentment at the person who had brought him to court, but he turned a deaf ear to their pleas. His appetite left him, his breath became foul, his digestion became bad, his sleeping habits were disturbed, and he lost over 16 lb in weight. Soon his heart and kidneys began to fail. He lost the lawsuit, and within a week was dead.

Of course, not all resentments have such a devastating effect. But you can be sure, they have *some* effect. It may not show up in the way I have just described, but it throws the internal machinery out of gear. Hate and resentment throws sand in the machinery of living.

David Seabury, a family doctor, says, 'Experience shows that pressure of undrained, wounded emotion plays a great part in creating fatigue, nervousness and worry even in youthful days.'

A missionary held a lifelong resentment against his mother, justifying it because of the treatment he had received from her. But that did not save him from a mental breakdown through the conflict that was set up in his soul.

Resentments are just as deadly in Christians as in non-Christians, though resentments have no place in a Christian's heart. Paul urges us never to let the sun go down on our wrath (Eph 4:26). If we go to sleep with resentment in our heart it will not only corrode the soul, but interfere with our physical functioning.

There is only one thing to do—forgive. We must forgive anyone who hurts us or injures us. And not only forgive them, but tell them so. The telling will be the catharsis, the cleansing.

Just as our negative attitudes can make us sick and unwell so our positive attitudes can make us well. Viktor Frankl, the famous doctor and psychiatrist who spent some years in German concentration camps, concluded after his ordeal that where there is a driving passion or a great purpose in life, the physical body is more likely to survive.

When he and a number of other doctors were inmates at Auschwitz during the Second World War, they observed that survival did not appear to depend on a person's physical constitution, but on their *will* to live. Often they saw the strong and healthy die, while some of the old and frail would survive. Those who did survive had some *reason* for living.

You, if you are a Christian, have the greatest reason for living. It is to share Christ's love with those around you. The areas I have covered in this chapter are those of attitudes that need to be chosen if we are to enjoy health and wholeness. Make sure these attitudes are part of your lifestyle, and God will guide you towards others.

10 Keeping the Temple in Good Repair

In the first epistle to the Corinthians, the apostle Paul says: 'Do you not know that your body is a temple of the Holy Spirit, who is in you, whom you have received from God? You are not your own; you were bought at a price. *Therefore honour God with your body*' (6:19–20, NIV, author's italics).

Could the matter be put more clearly? The Christian's body belongs to God. It is *his* property, and we are expected to pay as much concern to its welfare and upkeep as we would to the building in which we worship God every Sunday.

Paul has some strong words to those who treat the body with disrespect. 'Don't you know that you yourselves are God's temple and that God's Spirit lives in you? If anyone destroys God's temple, God will destroy him; for God's temple is sacred, and *you* are that temple' (1 Cor 3:16–17, NIV).

And just so that we don't miss the point, Paul says again in 2 Corinthians 6:16, 'For we are the temple of the living God' (NIV).

Think of it! Our bodies are the dwelling places of the Holy Spirit's presence. We are the custodians of the Lord's property. So take a good long honest look at your body right now.

Are you caring for it in such a way that it truly glorifies and honours God? Is it·a *fit* place for the Lord of glory to dwell?

Could the writer of Deuteronomy have been describing you when he wrote, 'Thou art waxen fat, thou art grown thick, thou art covered with fatness' (Deut 32:15, AV)?

God expects us to care for our bodies in the same way that we care for our spirits, and we shall have to give an account to him for both. It is my conviction that thousands of Christians have died before their time because they have failed to keep their bodies in proper repair.

You and I have a responsibility to keep our bodies in the best shape we can, barring accidents and genetic failure, of course, and to stay as long as possible on this earth, sharing the love of Jesus with our friends and families.

What are some of the things we should pay attention to in order to fulfil our obligations to our heavenly Landlord? In this chapter, I want to focus on what I consider the main ingredients of good physical care and preservation.

Watch what you eat

'Tell me what you eat,' said Brillat Savarin, 'and I will tell you what you are.' Experts in physical health tell us that what we eat plays a tremendous part in keeping the body healthy.

Thousands of years ago a Chinese doctor said that the body's only source of energy was the air breathed and the food eaten. One would assume, quite logically I believe, that with increased knowledge and the advances we have made in the twentieth century, that efforts would be made to avoid polluting the air and to make our food more nutritious. Regrettably, the very opposite is true.

We live in an age that, generally speaking, denies the body what it needs to maintain good health. Sometimes when I visit the local supermarket with my wife, I see couples with their trolleys piled high with what they consider are 'goodies'.

Most of the stuff in the packets and tins may look appealing and appetizing, but contains little nutrition. Nutrition, as you know, is the business of nourishing the cells of the body. What many housewives don't realize is that most of the nourishment has been taken out of much of the food they buy. It is practically valueless as far as the body's needs are concerned.

People sometimes comment on others: 'They certainly eat well.' But do they? Eating well means several things:

1. *Getting the right nutrition*

Many modern foods lack nutritional value partly because of the preservatives that are added. Our food was designed by God who meant us to eat it as close to the natural state as possible. The fruits, grains and vegetables were meant to absorb from the soil and the air the elements necessary to keep us in health. And they would do if we didn't destroy them before they get to our mouths by modern processing.

The sugar, rice, cereals and flour most people buy are stripped of nutrients and vitamins. While most of the people in the Western hemisphere walk around with full stomachs, they are starving to death nutritionally.

2. *Maintaining a balanced diet*

It is not within the scope of this chapter to prescribe diets. There's no need, for there are a great number of good books, written by experts, already available on this subject. I believe that every Christian owes it to the Lord to acquaint himself with information on how to eat properly.

We live in a dangerous age as far as our eating is concerned because the modern tendency is to concentrate on taste rather than on what is beneficial. Some people are sick simply because they feed off 'sick' food. Someone has said that we live off half we eat and the doctor lives off the other half.

When I try telling some Christians that they should cut down on such things as fried foods, black coffee, tea, hotdogs, pizzas, hamburgers, and so on, they can't believe that all that 'good' food is bad for them. The truth is, they are, as one doctor described it, digging their graves with their teeth.

Don't just sit there—exercise

Doctors' opinions vary about exercise. Dr Theodore Klumpp says: 'The activity should be something a person likes, such as golf, swimming, hiking, gardening or tennis.'

Dr Howard Ross says, 'Every muscle and joint that has the power to wiggle must be made to wiggle more.' All those who maintain that exercise is important to one's health emphasize one solid principle—*the body must be moved and moved regularly*.

I'm amazed at the antipathy many Christians have towards exercise. They shrug off their responsibility to keep the Lord's temple in good working order by such jokes as: 'Whenever I feel the need to exercise, I go and lie down until it goes away.'

Some quote Paul's statement: 'Bodily exercise profiteth little' (1 Tim 4:8, AV). However, let me quote his words from the Amplified Version: 'For physical training is of some value—useful for a little: but godliness (spiritual training) is useful and of value in everything...'

Paul is simply comparing here bodily exercise with spiritual exercise, and he is saying that spiritual training is far more beneficial in comparison to physical training. He is *not* saying that physical exercise is pointless and unnecessary.

Besides, in the days of the apostles, there was hardly any need for physical training or exercise. Most of them got all they needed by walking to wherever they had to go. It is recorded in Acts 20:13 that Paul chose to walk from Troas to Assos (a distance of about 15 miles) while the other disciples went by boat. The Amplified Bible says: 'intending himself to go by land—on foot'.

Too much mustn't be made of this, of course, but I can't help wondering whether Paul walked the 15-mile journey rather than go by boat because he felt the exercise might do him good!

Years ago, when people had operations, they were told not to move for a few days—sometimes weeks. Today it is different. Not long after an operation (usually the next day), someone will come to your bed and insist on you getting up.

Doctors have discovered that movement hastens healing. Not only that, but digestion and elimination will be much better, too, and it helps prevent the risk of embolism.

If you went to bed and stayed there without getting up for a week, you'd be amazed at the serious change in your body. Your muscles would have grown weak, your joints would have stiffened, your bowels would have clogged and your sense of balance would be affected.

There is danger in idleness. I don't know of any Christian who would go to bed deliberately, just in order to let his body go to pot. No one would do that deliberately. Yet I know of many who allow the same thing to take place slowly, over a long period of time, by not taking sufficient exercise. The lack of exercise has the same effect as spending a long time in bed. The only difference being that it takes longer for the damage to occur.

About eight years ago I went to my doctor, complaining of tiredness. After examining me thoroughly, he said that there was nothing wrong with me, and that I probably needed to slow up. I knew that wasn't the answer because I was working well within my capacity, but then a friend suggested to me that I ought to consider a programme of physical exercise.

I looked into this, reading every book I could find on the subject, and began, slowly at first, to develop a system of daily exercises. I bought an exercise bicycle, did some stretching, bending and so on, and within a few weeks, the difference was positively amazing. Speaking for myself, I am convinced that daily physical exercise helped me to maintain my output for God, and my contribution to his kingdom, as much as prayer, meditation and other spiritual exercises.

I know from experience that whenever my output is below its normal level, it is usually because I have not kept up my proper programme of exercises. There may be other reasons, of course, but *usually* it is due to my inattention to my personal fitness programme.

You are fortunate if you have a job that calls for physical activity. You may not feel the need for further exercise. However, if you are an office worker, sitting all day at a desk, use every opportunity you can to get up and walk about. But even if you have a job that calls for physical activity, vigorous exercise now and again is beneficial. A fast walk, jogging, cycling, playing tennis, etc., forces blood to the farthest extremities of your body, into the tiny capillaries, carrying its life-giving load to, and restoring, the decadent cells.

Two cautions, however. Don't do strenuous exercise immediately after a meal, and, if in doubt about your health, have a medical check-up before starting on a strenuous exercise programme. Indeed, build up gradually from gentle to more strenuous exercises.

Just as the condition of the mind greatly affects the body, so does the condition of the body affect the mind. It is essential that we do with our bodies what God intended us to do—move them. The principle is quite simple—we either activate or disintegrate. So don't just sit there—exercise!

Watch your weight

Are you one of those overweight people, living what someone described as a life of quiet desperation? Then you've got company. Medical experts tell us that being overweight is the nation's number one health problem.

But losing weight, getting down to what the tables call 'our ideal weight', can be frustrating. The ads say: 'Feel great, lose weight.' It's easier said than done. We will feel better *after* we have lost weight, but losing it (or trying to) often feels like physical torture.

There can be little doubt that some people's weight problems are inherited. 'The sure way to prevent obesity,' said someone, 'is to look around for parents of slender build nine months before you are born.' There may be little we can do to prevent a predisposition to obesity, but there is a lot we can do to prevent a predisposition becoming a reality.

I have the kind of body that, unless I eat the right foods, soon puts on extra weight. A few years ago, I was a good deal overweight so I sat down to work out a system for reducing weight and keeping myself in trim. I'd like to share it with you.

1. *Offer a prayer to God for his help as you begin*

This puts you in the right frame of mind and puts the whole matter into perspective. After all, your body doesn't belong to you, but to God. Making a commitment in prayer underlines it as being more than a physical matter but a spiritual one.

Charlie Shedd, an American preacher and author, says that when he fell on his knees with one hundred and twenty pounds too much fat on his body, acknowledged his responsibility and asked for God's help to put things right, he heard the Lord saying to him, 'You've come to the right place.' Prayer is like a sculptor surrendering his chisel so that he stops chipping away at his own wants. The tools must be turned over to God. For, as Charlie Shedd says: 'The fat is not only in your body, it's also in your head.'

2. *Ask yourself: why do I overeat?*

There are many reasons why people overeat: emotional needs, feelings of inadequacy, disappointment, anger, boredom, frustration. These and many other feelings can send people scurrying for food and its physical solace. In my case, the trigger to overeat is when I face writing deadlines. Then I tend to rely on food as a cushion for my tense feelings.

But I have discovered that once you trace the reason for overeating, it loses a lot of its hold upon you. Experts who have studied the subject say that the biggest single reason for overeating is the way an individual perceives himself. In other words, our self-image. It might sound a little frightening, but in most cases it is true—scratch a fat person and you find an emotional problem.

How do you feel about yourself? Do you feel glad you are *you*? Or do you wish you were somebody else? Chances are that if you are not happy about yourself, then you will overeat to cushion the negative feelings that are reverberating inside you. The conflicting emotions must be brought to the peace table and dealt with, because if not, then they can make you hungry.

3. *Decide, with God's help, tc discipline your appetite*

T. K. Chamber, writing in 1850, said: 'The hourly watch over the instinctive desires, which must be observed by one desirous of reducing his corpulence, makes it a solemn thing. He that commences it must . . . mount guard and lie in constant ambush against himself.'

Self-supervision or self-discipline is a solemn thing, and it doesn't come easily. Keep in mind, however, that you are a disciple of Christ, and remember that his words 'If anyone would come after me, he must deny himself' (Mt 16:24, NIV) apply as much to what you put into your mouth as to what you put into your mind.

One man who was overweight and knew that God wanted him to do something about it, turned to his Bible and asked God for guidance. The text he opened the Bible at was this: 'Watch and pray, that ye enter not into temptation' (Mt 26:41, AV). In the fight against flab, the word *watch* is as important as the word *pray*.

Discipline involves being a disciple of Christ and, quite simply, being a disciple means paying more attention to God than to food. Are you willing to be that kind of disciple?

4. *Understand the basic principle of losing weight*

Weight is determined by the number of calories you put into your body, balanced against the number you expend. Less food reduces the intake. Greater body activity increases the output. The best thing, of course, is to combine the two.

But unless you realize that, basically, there has to be reduced food intake in order to lose weight, then you will be at the mercy of the advertisements that promise you all kinds of physical rewards if you invest your money in their products.

Speaking for myself, a guaranteed way to lose weight is to limit myself to about 1,250 calories a day. That way I can predict a loss of one pound every other day. Some might discover that a low-carbohydrate diet is better than just counting calories. But whatever approach you use, remember you can't lose weight and keep it off unless you eat fewer calories than you expend.

5. *Meditate on those scriptures that underline a Christian's responsibility to his body*

Keeping appropriate texts from Scripture in one's mind when seeking to build up resistance against overeating, is something that has never been fully explored. The following scriptures are just a few that I keep before me, and meditate on, whenever I am tempted to overeat. They have worked for me. I believe they will work for you:

'Each of you should learn to control his own body' (1 Thess 4:4, NIV).
'Those who live according to the flesh set their minds on the things of the flesh' (Rom 8:5, RSV).
'I beseech you...brethren...present your bodies a living sacrifice...unto God, which is your reasonable service' (Rom 12:1, AV).
'Here is my advice. Live your whole life in the Spirit and you will not satisfy the desires of your lower nature' (Gal 5:16, PHILLIPS).

Learn to relax

Several years ago I attended a conference in the United States which was for the purpose of helping ministers improve their effectiveness in the area of Christian leadership. Imagine my surprise when, on the first morning, it was announced that before the ministry of the word, everyone would be expected to participate in a relaxation class.

I don't mind telling you, I felt a little peeved. I had come a distance of 4,000 miles to increase my effectiveness as a minister and a counsellor, and I was eager to get started in one of the various workshops that had been advertised.

But those early morning relaxation classes did more for me than all the workshops put together. I learned something in them that has helped me put into practice, day by day, a simple programme of relaxation.

The first thing I was told was that ministers are notoriously bad at relaxing. They think they are relaxed when they are not. This point was proved when we were told to lie on the floor, whereupon the instructor came round to each of us, lifting various arms or legs to show just how tense we really were. And this, despite the fact that each person said they felt fairly relaxed.

Before we can learn to relax, we were told we must first be able to recognize tension. We acquire such a habit of muscle tension over the years and are so accustomed to it, that we are unaware of inappropriate contraction of the muscles.

We were then put through a systematic routine of contracting each group of muscles in the body, in turn, then releasing the tension. We were told, for example, to screw up our faces as tightly as we could, hold them in that position for a few moments, then quickly relax.

Then the same with the neck, the shoulders, the arms and so on, until every major part of the body was covered.

The strong contractions, that is, deliberately tensing the various muscles, certainly helped us to recognize the difference between tension and relaxation.

Now, whenever I feel tense, I lie down, and, starting with my feet, I go through each group of muscles in my body, contracting then relaxing them. It's positively amazing the effect this has upon one physically. Believe me, relaxation techniques work.

One well-known American minister, who was at the conference I attended, and who pastored a church of several thousand people, said that before he came to the conference his doctor had told him that he was facing a severe breakdown in his health. During the relaxation classes, he became aware of the frantic pace of his life: the endless committee meetings, the preparation of so many addresses, the frequent trips by air from one city to another, working all hours of the day and night. He decided, then and there, that he would re-evaluate his priorities, and either delegate the non-essentials or cut them out altogether.

I heard nothing more about the minister until just recently when I picked up an American magazine that contained an article written by him, entitled, 'I was all set for a breakdown–then God taught me to relax'.

In the article he said: 'For years I wondered why I found it difficult to meditate on the Scriptures. Others spoke about meditation and its benefits, but I could never sit quietly in a room and focus on a single text for more than a few seconds at a time. Then someone taught me how to relax. When I learned how to physically relax, let the tensions in my body go, the spin-off was this—I became more relaxed in mind. Now I find that I can meditate, not for minutes, but for hours.'

Relaxation is a good common-sense way of dealing with the stresses and pressures of life. And it's no good saying we ought to be spiritual enough not to need the benefits of relaxation. The simple fact is we do get caught up in the pressures of today's world, and a few simple relaxation exercises can help relieve muscular tension.

Try it. I'll be surprised if it doesn't help.

Sleep well!

No one really knows what sleep is, or exactly what causes it, or why it is needed. All we know is that if we don't get the right amount of it, or the right type of sleep, we are in serious trouble.

Sleep acts as a generator that charges the battery of our bodies. It is as important as nutritious food, exercise, fresh air and right thinking. For many years, most doctors and scientists believed that sleep requirements varied with each person, so that no one could say how much sleep an individual needed in order to live and work at his peak.

Today, research workers are sure that variation among individuals is considerably less than they once thought. One doctor says: 'The pace and stress of modern life has increased the importance of getting enough sleep. All human beings need a minimum of six hours if they are to be mentally alert and healthy. Most people need more. Those who think they can make do with less are fooling themselves.'

Some years ago, I attempted to find out my own sleep cycle. I discovered, after several weeks of experimenting, that I needed eight hours' sleep if I was to be of maximum effectiveness. Now I try to make sure that I get that amount—no matter what happens.

Lack of sleep can make normally cheerful people feel

moody and depressed. Intensified by still more lack of sleep, these signs of inner distress may spread like an infection into the symptoms of mental illness. Significant sleep loss is a subtle poison.

One authority on the subject puts it simply: 'If we do not get enough sleep, we cannot be fully awake during the day.' This is dangerous, because if we are not fully awake, then we are not in our right minds. And if we are not in our right minds, how can we be our best for God?

Some years ago, some studies were made of two schizophrenic patients, who had suffered extreme sleeplessness during a certain period, and of several medical students, who were experimentally deprived of sleep. The doctors who observed them reported: 'Many agitated persons on the brink of a psychotic breakdown suffer from severe insomnia...a few pass through a prolonged period of wakefulness as the schizophrenic process unfolds.'

Whether sleep loss is a cause or an effect of the breakdown is not entirely clear, but it *does* appear to be part of the process. For this reason, anyone who simultaneously undergoes anxiety and sleep loss may be heading for trouble.

Many authorities also tell us that two hours' sleep before midnight is equivalent to four hours afterwards. It seems that as night comes on, and we revolve away from the sun, there is an almost mystic pull from mother earth that induces sleep to restore man's mental and physical powers. The old adage: 'Early to bed, early to rise, makes a man healthy, wealthy and wise' is more than just a pithy saying. It makes sense.

Millions of people stay up late simply out of habit. Many feel that the late evening hours are the only ones they can call their own. Some stay up late because they are dissatisfied with how little they have accomplished during the day. The irony is that if they got the sleep they needed, their days might be better balanced. Others stay up because of worries and anxieties. Still others think that time spent in sleep is lost.

A Christian has a nightcap that is not available to anyone else. He can balance the ledger at the end of each day in the presence of God. He can lay his anxieties to rest in the arms of the Almighty, and go to sleep in the consciousness that God is in control of his life and that he is the personal responsibility of the Creator.

A peaceful sleep will not come, however, unless a Christian obeys the injunction that says: 'Let not the sun go down upon your wrath' (Eph 4:26). All resentments, jealousy or bitterness that may have accumulated during the day must be unloaded in his presence. A Christian may sleep without following such a procedure, but it will not be a healthy sleep.

We need to consider one more thing if we are to enjoy the blessing of a peaceful and healthy sleep, and that is to do a good day's work, as if we are working for the Lord, for the 'sleep of a labouring man is sweet' (Eccles 5:12).

The Psalmist reminds us that when we trust him as our 'Watchman', not just the locks on our doors or the dog in the yard, then we will have no need of sleeping pills or tranquillizers, for 'he giveth his beloved sleep' (Ps 127:2).

Are the results of taking care of God's temple, and treating it with the respect it deserves, worth it? The answer is a resounding *yes*. In addition to improved appearance, new buoyancy and greater effectiveness, you will have a gratifying sense that you have fulfilled your responsibility as the caretaker of God's temple.

One writer says: 'We cannot be responsible for the body we begin life with, but we are responsible for the one we die with.' The body can be improved, no matter how handicapped it may have been in the beginning.

Dr Stanley Jones, the famous missionary to India, said: 'I have lived for thirty-five years in one of the worst climates of the world—India, a land poverty-stricken and disease-ridden—"the white man's grave". And yet I have come out of it at the end of these years with a better body than I had when I went in.'

If every Christian was to give the body its rightful care and consideration then, instead of going to heaven before our time, we would be able to share God's love with our friends and families, and the community in which we live, and thus fulfil our mission on this earth.

The choice of living your allotted span is not entirely in God's hands. It is in your hands too. This is the mystery of the divine human partnership. You have a choice—a powerful choice.

Choose life!

Also by the same author in Kingsway paperback . . .

Marriage As God Intended

by Selwyn Hughes

'We have never had an argument in the whole of our marriage,' said the husband.
'How did you accomplish that?' asked the counsellor.
'We just don't talk.'

Communication is only one of the problem areas faced by married couples—there can be many other difficulties that cause us to fall short of God's perfect plan.

This book offers help—not only with specific problems, but for improving what is already good and healthy.

There are chapters on:
> relationships with parents and in-laws
> who's the head of the family?
> sexual difficulties
> the temptation to adultery
> divorce and remarriage

Selwyn Hughes is highly respected as a leading marriage guidance counsellor. Here he draws on his many years' experience as both husband and counsellor, blending biblical principles with practical suggestions on how to let God keep your marriage at its best.

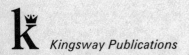

Kingsway Publications

Available from your usual Christian book supplier, or Mail Order enquiries to: Charisma Christian Mail Order, P.O. Box 77, Hailsham, E. Sussex BN27 3EF.

A Friend in Need
how to help people through their problems

by Selwyn Hughes

John is unable to overcome his feelings of
bitterness and resentment. Anita knows her
depression is not physically caused, but she is
powerless to do anything about it. Brian is
fighting a losing battle with impure thoughts.
Like thousands of others in trouble they need
to be shown simple scriptural principles that
can set them right.

Selwyn Hughes believes that helping people
through their problems is not simply the task
of ministers and trained counsellors. If you are
a Christian, then you are in a position to help
others. This book provides guidelines which
you can begin to use right away to help people
you know overcome their difficulties.

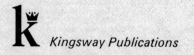

Kingsway Publications

Available from your usual
Christian book supplier, or
Mail Order enquiries to:
Charisma Christian Mail Order,
P.O. Box 77, Hailsham,
E. Sussex BN27 3EF.

How to Live the Christian Life

by Selwyn Hughes
author of *Every Day with Jesus*

Do you
wish the day was over before it has hardly
begun?
get irritated by even the smallest problems?
find reading the Bible every day difficult
and tiresome?
have trouble mastering temptation?
try to copy others instead of developing
your own gifts?

We can cram our heads with doctrine, but
that in itself will not keep us from the problems
that rob our lives of the peace, joy and
effectiveness that Jesus promised. This book
points the way through such problems,
helping us to become the kind of people God
intended. It is a positive affirmation that we
can get the best out of the Christian life.

Kingsway Publications

A New Heart
The promise of God to those who believe

by Selwyn Hughes

Is a victorious Christian life possible? Can we know power and purity in our lives, and real faith?

Selwyn Hughes shows how God desires to win our hearts and so enable us to turn his promises into reality.

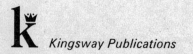

Kingsway Publications

Available from your usual Christian book supplier, or Mail Order enquiries to: Charisma Christian Mail Order, P.O. Box 77, Hailsham, E. Sussex BN27 3EF.

The Christian Counsellor's Pocket Guide

by Selwyn Hughes

Have you ever been asked for help, or confronted with a challenge, only to find that your resources amount to little more than 'I think it says somewhere in the Bible...'?

Selwyn Hughes believes that no Christian need find himself in this position, and has therefore compiled this handbook of Bible references and practical advice after many years' experience in the counselling ministry.

Section A deals with the most common problems that trouble Christians;

Section B deals with objections raised by many unbelievers;

Section C confronts the most frequent intellectual excuses given as barriers to personal commitment.

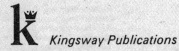

Kingsway Publications

Available from your usual
Christian book supplier, or
Mail Order enquiries to:
Charisma Christian Mail Order,
P.O. Box 77, Hailsham,
E. Sussex BN27 3EF.

Every Day *Reflections*

by Selwyn Hughes

This collection of daily readings for the whole year covers a wide range of topics to help Christians everywhere on the road to full maturity.

The readings have been selected from *Every Day With Jesus*, the increasingly popular devotional aid released every two months by the Crusade for World Revival.

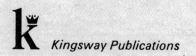
Kingsway Publications

Available from your usual
Christian book supplier, or
Mail Order enquiries to:
Charisma Christian Mail Order,
P.O. Box 77, Hailsham,
E. Sussex BN27 3EF.